# The Voice
## in the
# Laburnum
# Tree

Gloria Kearney

**AMBASSADOR INTERNATIONAL**
Greenville, South Carolina • Belfast, Northern Ireland

THE VOICE IN THE LABURNUM TREE
© Copyright 2007 Gloria Kearney

Cover photo by N Vandergaag
(Van Dusen Botanical Garden, Vancouver)

ISBN 978-1-84030-190-8


Ambassador Publications
a division of
Ambassador Productions Ltd.
Providence House
Ardenlee Street,
Belfast,
BT6 8QJ
Northern Ireland
www.ambassador-productions.com

Emerald House
427 Wade Hampton Blvd.
Greenville
SC 29609, USA
www.emeraldhouse.com

# A Word of
# Thanks

THANKS FROM GLORIA:

to my wonderful, long-suffering family who put up with an untidy house and scrappy meals while I wrote this story - I promise we'll have a roast dinner one of these days!

to Lavinia, Gwen and Pat, my friends and prayer partners, who encouraged me to keep going – you must have wondered if I would ever get it finished!

to Janet, Pat Logan's daughter-in-law, who spent many hours typing up Pat's stories to provide me with a basis for the book – that was a labour of love!

to Christine and Pat who proof read the manuscript – what eagle eyes you have! ( not Pat Logan, but Pat my prayer partner – there are too many Pats on this page!)

to everyone at Ambassador – for agreeing to publish the book and for waiting patiently for it to be completed

## THANKS FROM PAT:

to my wonderful God, who called me to write this book as a testimony to my grandchildren and others

to Dr Gilbert Egerton – when I was overwhelmed at this calling, you so encouraged my heart by saying, 'My dear, anyone can get education but it is experience that counts and you have experienced God.'

to my dearest daughter, Janet – I cannot call you daughter-in-law! Your loving, caring spirit has been so appreciated, as has all your hard work on the book. You are a great blessing to me and also to Hugh – thank you, dear

to all who have prayed for God's help and guidance in the completion of this book – your prayers have meant more than you know

to dear Sadie Graham, whom God chose to open doors that led me to Gloria, whom God then led to write the book

to Gloria – my grateful thanks. God has surely given you a special gift. God granted me the experiences but you have been able to write them in such a wonderful way, that I have thoroughly enjoyed reading them all again!

to my husband, Hugh – only you (and the Lord) really know what I have gone through in the writing of this book. I sincerely thank you for your patience, love and prayers. Guess what you are getting for Christmas?

# List of
# Contents

## Prologue
# Let it Be to Me ...

IT WAS THE great Day of Assignments and I had been summoned by the King to stand, with many others, before the Throne. As I waited in the long line, the Master drew alongside and whispered in my ear,
"The King has a special assignment for you."
My heart leapt with gladness and I began to wonder what it might be. I longed to serve the Great King and I determined that however difficult this assignment might be, I would tackle it with vigour and enthusiasm.
I listened intently as others were given their assignments.
"You will carry My word to unreached places in China," He announced to one young man.
What an amazing assignment! I turned to the Master with great excitement.
"I could do something like that........ be a missionary in a far off land. Will that be my task too?"
The Master smiled, "Be patient..... soon you will find out...... just wait and see."

Again the voice of the Great King thundered from the Throne,

"You will serve Me by serving the poor and the outcasts."

I knew that such work was very dear to the heart of the Master and I felt a yearning in my heart for a similar assignment. The Master felt my yearning too but just placed His hand on my shoulder and softly reassured me,

"The Great King knows best. He has an assignment that is just right for you."

I listened again as a young girl in a nurse's uniform took her turn before the Throne.

"You will show My love to the sick, the distressed and the dying," declared the Great King.

"Oh now, I could do that," I whispered quickly to the Master. "I could train to be a nurse too. I could share His love . . . . . ."

The Master put His finger to His lips,

"Shush Child, your assignment has already been decided. Don't try to take on someone else's."

So I waited quietly before the Throne until the Great King beckoned me to draw near. My heart pounded and my legs trembled as I approached His Presence.

His voice rang out.

"I have called you to be My handmaiden."

His handmaiden? What sort of an assignment was that? I turned to the Master in some confusion. I could always be totally honest with Him so I voiced my disappointment.

"I was expecting a great assignment. The people before me were given important jobs to do. Is the Great King not pleased with me? Have I offended Him in some way? Why am I to be just a handmaiden?"

The Master's gentle look of reproach was enough to stem the flow of protest.

"Oh Child, how little you understand," He said softly. "The King chooses His handmaidens from those who are closest to His heart. He calls them to an intimacy that many never know, even some of these who are assigned what appear to be the important tasks. His handmaidens stay close enough to hear His Voice clearly and learn to do His bidding instantly. Their calling is to serve humbly, to obey completely, to love passionately until the time comes when they can sense the very heartbeat of the Great King, can catch a glimpse of His purposes in the world. Then they can pray His Kingdom into being on the earth."

"Oh, I didn't understand," I cried, feeling ashamed. The tears welled up and I fell to my knees before the Throne. What an honour, what an immense privilege to be His handmaiden. This was surely the best assignment of all and I determined there and then to listen intently for His Voice. I dared to raise my eyes to meet the gaze of the Great King and the brilliance of His loving smile flooded my whole being.

"Let it be to me," I whispered, "according to Your word."

## Chapter 1
# No Ordinary Arrival

12th MARCH, 1938

The ambulance screeched to a halt outside Lewisham Hospital in London and the waiting Matron hurried towards it, pushing a wheelchair into place at the back door. Six nurses rushed over to help the heavily pregnant woman into the wheelchair. The woman moaned and immediately tried to lift herself off the seat.

"No! No! Sit still," shouted the Matron, pushing her back down into the chair.

"But the baby's head is out!" protested the distressed patient.

Matron knew she had to act quickly and shouted to the nurses,

"Make a bed with your arms. There's no time – the baby has arrived!"

So, as May lay uncomfortably on the nurses' arms, Pat Hyde made her entrance into the world – a tiny four and a half pound baby.

She had no name for a day or two, despite several suggestions made by Auntie Eileen and friends who came to admire the new arrival. May enjoyed listening to the radio and one afternoon heard the presenter say,

"Now we have Pat Hyde, the singer, to sing to you ….."

The rest of the announcement went unheard as May realised that she liked the singer's name -

"That's what we'll call her – Pat Hyde."

She shared her idea with her husband when he came to visit and he agreed with her plan.

"Let's also name her after her dead grandmothers – Esther and Sarah."

May thought that would be lovely but somehow Patricia Esther Sarah Hyde seemed to be rather a mouthful for the tiny baby lying in the hospital cot so they combined the two middle names to Essa – Es for Esther and Sa for Sarah.

May and Joseph, her husband, were originally from Northern Ireland. They grew up in the same neighbourhood and married in St Jude's Church of Ireland, on the Ormeau Road, Belfast, in 1928. Times were hard and jobs were few, so Joseph moved his family over to London so that he could take up a position in Joseph's brother's French polishing business. When things didn't work out in the business, he decided to go into painting and decorating.

When they brought their little daughter home, there were two excited brothers waiting to see her – Joseph (or Joe, as he came to be known) who was five and Richard Harold who was three. May used to smile as she watched Joe singing to his sister – one of his favourite songs was "Jesus wants me for a sunbeam". Life was good just then but she was not to know that dark clouds were looming on the horizon – clouds that would shatter that perfect little family.

One Friday, when Pat was about two years old, Joe suddenly took ill. When the usual remedies didn't help to reduce his fever, they sent for a doctor, who had him rushed to hospital. He was quickly diagnosed with a new disease, meningitis, and the doctors began a frantic battle to save his life. On Monday, Joseph and May were sitting outside the double-doors of the ward, waiting to go to see their little boy, when May felt a sudden swish of wind sweeping past her, moving towards the doors and beyond.

"Joey's dead," she announced as she turned to her husband. No sooner had she spoken than the doors opened and a grim faced doctor came to speak to them.

"I'm terribly sorry," he said, "but your little son has passed away. We would like to ask for your help – meningitis is new to us and we would like your permission to use your son's body for research, in order to be able to save others."

It was a difficult decision to make but the thought that other children might be saved and other parents spared this ordeal encouraged them to agree to the suggestion.

May was still living under the cloud of grief when she was overshadowed by another huge cloud - the outbreak of the Second World War. Joseph, like so many of his friends, felt compelled to answer the call to arms in defence of his country and arrived home one day with the news that he had joined up. So May was left all alone to grieve for her dead child and to bring up her three year old son and her new little baby daughter. The future stretched out uncertainly before her – would she be able to manage on her own? .......... would the war be lost and life be changed forever? ........... would Joseph ever come home from the war? .........would he be the same person who had left with such determination to play his part in the conflict?

In those uncertain days, it was a comfort to her to remember the things she had learnt in the Gospel Hall and Salvation Army meetings she had attended as a child – about a God who loved the world, who cared for ordinary people, who wanted to connect with them, to listen to their prayers and forgive their sin. She was greatly touched when that same God reached out to her in a very special way. May called in to a café one day for a cup of tea, bringing Harold and Pat with her. She hardly noticed the other lady sitting at a nearby table, so she was very surprised when the lady came over and said,

"I believe God would have me give you this Bible for your little daughter."

There was a warm feeling in May's heart as she watched the woman place a beautiful large black Bible on the table. She asked what the baby's name was and then carefully wrote Pat's name and the date on the front page.

Little Pat experienced that same warm feeling in later years when she would take the Bible out to look at it and hear her Mum tell the story again. She was too young to fully appreciate that she was holding the very Word of God in her hand, but she was intrigued by it – she loved to hear the rustle of the fine paper as she turned the pages and she was constantly amazed that this beautiful book belonged to her! She could have had no idea that the Bible would become so precious to her in years to come, that she would live her life by its teachings, find comfort and peace in its pages and learn to love and worship its author.

## Chapter 2
# A New Home in London

THE EARLY YEARS of the war were dangerous and difficult for May and her little family, but even in the midst of the fierce bombing, God's hand of protection was on their lives. It seemed to Pat that each time her Mum decided to travel out of London to Uncle Billy in Scotland or to the family back in Northern Ireland, they would return to find that the house they had been living in had been bombed. At the time, of course, Pat was much too young to appreciate the full horror of those years, but she would remember it as a time of confusion and bewilderment, of long, uncomfortable journeys, of tension and tears at home, of loud noises in the night.

She would remember too the traumatic experience of evacuation. May became seriously ill and was rushed into hospital. It was decided that the best thing to do would be to evacuate the children, so Harold and Pat, at six and three and a half years old, were sent to a family in Tunbridge Wells. In that home, where they should have been assured of love and care, they were mentally abused.

On one occasion, May sent them a parcel of oranges and chocolates, both scarce commodities. The couple and their fifteen year old son took great delight in sitting at the dining table and calling Harold and Pat to join them.

"Do you like oranges?" they asked.

"Yes," the children answered, very quietly.

"Then watch us eat them!" came the cruel reply.

They then went through the same procedure with the chocolates, eating all that had been sent, while Pat and Harold received nothing and could only sit watching while their mouths watered at the sight of the goodies.

The son was extremely devious and would continually get Harold into trouble by encouraging the six year old into situations that he knew were wrong. He would then stand back and laugh while Harold received a thrashing for what had been done. One evening before dinner the children ran outside to the back yard to go to the toilet and wash their hands, as the couple insisted they did before each meal. The son deliberately stayed in the toilet to stop Harold and Pat using it.

"Please, please!" the little ones pleaded.

"You're not getting in! You're going to get a thrashing!" the voice taunted from the other side of the door.

Suddenly the father's voice yelled out angrily from the kitchen. Harold was so startled and frightened that he wet himself. When the father realised what had happened, instead of being sympathetic, he stripped all the clothes off Harold and then proceeded to beat his naked body black and blue with a leather strap. Pat will never forget the awfulness of those moments, as she stood there helplessly and listened to the frantic cries of her brother.

Despite the awful treatment he was enduring, little Harold showed a maturity beyond his years when they found out that May was coming to pay a visit. She had just been released from hospital after convalescing.

"If Mum asks if we're happy," he instructed his little sister, "say yes. She's sick and we don't want to worry her."

At last the long awaited day arrived – although it was wonderful to see Mum again, for Pat, the joy was tinged with fear that she would say the wrong thing and so incur Harold's wrath. It was a cool but sunny Spring day in April so May took the two children for a walk. The skirt of the grey coat she wore swung from side to side as they walked together. It wasn't long before the dreaded question was put to Harold.

"Are you happy here, son?" she enquired.

"Oh yes," he replied quickly, smiling up into her face.

Despite his confident reply, May was not convinced and turned to Pat, knowing that she was too young to bluff her.

"And what about you, Patsy? Are you happy?"

Pat looked fearfully at Harold, who shot her warning glances between each swing of the grey coat.

"Yes," she whispered – but her Mum had seen the truth in her eyes.

When she brought them back to the house, she demanded their belongings and, to the great relief of the children, returned with them to London.

This may have solved one problem but it also created another. Their home in London had been bombed and May had nowhere to bring her children. In the end, they stayed overnight with some friends. There was only one thing to do – contact Joseph in the Army. Fortunately, the Army granted him leave to find them a home – but only for 24 hours!

Once more, God worked on their behalf. Early that day, Joseph saw a notice in a shop window, advertising a flat for rent. Knowing that accommodation like that would be snapped up very quickly, he jumped on a bus right away and was able to secure it. May and the children walked to meet him at their new home – 76, Adelaide Avenue. The sun was shining and the birds seemed to be singing just for them as Joseph and May gazed at the lovely Victorian house, set in a tree-lined avenue and overlooked by a beautiful Grammar School that had been built high on the grassy slopes. This would be Pat's home until she was sixteen years old, a home that would hold many happy memories.

It was a tall house, with beautiful high ceilings and a centre rose in each room. Two of the reception rooms, with white marble fireplaces, were divided by heavy mahogany doors which could open up to make one huge room with bay windows at the front. There was a servants' bell in every room, servants' quarters at the top of the house and facilities for them to do washing and cooking in the basement. The big mahogany front door had a heavy brass knocker with a matching letterbox and key lock – it became Pat's job to polish these until they shone brightly.

At the back of the house were four steps leading up to Pat's bedroom, which had a verandah outside the window. She took great pleasure in stepping on to the verandah on sunny days to view all the surrounding gardens. They were all long and narrow and theirs had an apple tree at the bottom. The garden on the left had lots of fruit trees – apricots, greengages, cherries, apples, pears, peaches and plums. A massive yellow laburnum tree, with long trailing blooms grew in the garden on the right. The back gate of their house led on to Ivy Lane and an eight foot wall hid a cemetery. Although it was mostly obscured by trees, Pat could see it from her bedroom window. Directly below her verandah was a long sunny room with French doors that led into the garden.

All sorts of games were played in that lovely garden in the summer days but when the winter came and snow fell, Harold and Pat would take their toboggan up the grassy slopes, the "Hilly Fields". Their friends would join them as they sped faster and faster down the slippery slopes. It was a dangerous sport and quite a few children and even adults were killed when their toboggans careered into the path of oncoming traffic on Adelaide Avenue.

Pat's childhood in that lovely old house was colourful and exciting, the days full of love and laughter but the shadow of war was never far away. A Morrison shelter was set up in the room that had the French doors – it was built like a cage to protect the occupants from falling debris in the event of a bomb landing nearby. This became Pat and Harold's bedroom each night. Before going to sleep, they used to sing this little chorus:

"God is our refuge, don't be afraid,
He'll be with you all through the raid.
When bombs are falling and danger is near,
He will be with you until the 'All Clear'."

Pat's first public singing engagement came as a result of that song. The Presbyterian minister, who lived five doors away from Pat and her family, heard about the children singing and invited Pat to sing the chorus in the women's meeting. The women all sat in a circle and Pat stood on a chair in the middle, singing her heart out. The ladies seemed to be enthralled by this expression of faith in one so young.

They weren't the only occupants in the house – an elderly couple called Amy and George lived in the upper part. Little Pat was fascinated by them – Amy always wore black Victorian dresses that swished to the floor and black laced boots and stockings. George had a glass eye so Pat was never quite sure if he was looking directly at her or not. Before the Morrison shelter had been set up, the family had shared an Anderson shelter with Amy and George. There was something strangely comforting in hearing the little ritual the old couple carried out each time they settled to wait in the shelter:

"Are you alright, Amy?" George would ask.

"I'm alright, George," Amy would reply, "Are you alright, George?"

"I'm alright, Amy."

On one occasion, though, things were not "alright" for the siren went off in the daytime at a most inconvenient time – when Amy had just decided to have a bath! Pat and Harold were treated to the sight of a most dishevelled Amy, dripping with water, flying down the four flights of stairs in her effort to reach the shelter before the bombs would fall. On every flight of stairs she left a trail of clothes that she had just gathered up in the bathroom. Harold laughed out loud as he watched the thin white legs and bare feet of this refined Victorian lady as she sprinted to the place of safety.

"Look at old Amy!" he called to Pat. "Can't she fly!"

## Chapter 3
# The Blitz

HAROLD AND PAT were walking home, as they did every day in the early afternoon, from the infants' school near their home. They left the narrow railed walk that was Ivy Lane and turned onto Adelaide Avenue, following the line of the hedge surrounding a church that had recently been bombed. Suddenly, without any warning, a German plane, all guns blazing, swooped down towards the two children.

"Here's a Jerry plane!" shouted Harold, quickly grabbing Pat and throwing her into the hedge. Pat lay there with Harold's body protecting her, her head twisted on its side and pressed into the ground. She was able to peep under Harold's arm and was horrified to see the bullets pelting the pavement just inches from where he lay.

The plane passed over without harming them and then the sirens began to wail all around them. Other terrified, screaming children ran past them, unsure of what to do or where to go.

Meanwhile, Harold and Pat's Mum had heard the sirens and ran out on to the street to see if she could find her two children. She found herself surrounded by scores of hysterical children who had nowhere to hide. Her door was open and she hurriedly guided them inside, filling the rooms and landings with terrified children, at the same time frantically searching the street for signs of Harold and Pat. At last, just as the "All Clear" sounded, they arrived, white-faced and shaking. How relieved she was to see them and to know that God had kept them from harm!

The Blitz years were very traumatic. They never knew when their area would be the next target of Jerry's Doodlebugs. These flying bombs had no pilot and often (almost every day) flew over the eight foot wall at the bottom of their garden. The family would first of all be aware of a long, droning noise. Then there would be silence, a drawn out silence when everyone seemed to hold their breath and their hearts would race with fear. The silence would be broken by a deafening explosion and everyone would know that somewhere nearby, buildings had been destroyed and often lives lost as well.

A further, less serious consequence of the war was rationing. Coupons were distributed to everyone and had to be used to buy food or clothes. The availability of food was affected too – there were few sweets and little fruit. Many foods were just too expensive for the family to buy. Pat didn't taste banana, melon or coconut until after the war. Her diet consisted mainly of soup, bread, jam, spam and dripping. She always looked forward to Sunday dinner – it was the best meal of the week.

There was great excitement when one of the sweet shops replenished its stock. A long queue formed outside the door and from their place in the queue, Pat and Harold watched expectantly as the door opened, their mouths watering in anticipation. Pat clutched her two pennies tightly as the queue got closer to the door. Eventually they reached the counter, only to be told, "Sorry, sold out!" What a disappointment!

But life wasn't all danger and disappointments – there were lighter moments too. The two children enjoyed going to the cinema (or the pictures, as it was known). They sold lemonade bottles and jam jars to save the required nine pennies for the tickets, sixpennies for ice cream at the interval and three pennies for chips on the way home. Somehow chips eaten straight from the greaseproof paper and newspaper wrapping seemed to taste better than any other way of serving them! Treats like this didn't happen too often.

The arrival of their Uncle Dick, Joseph's youngest brother, always brought fun and laughter into their lives. He would visit them when he got leave from the Army.

"Come and play with us, Uncle Dick," the children would shout.

"I'm going to chase you all over the house and jump that 8 foot cemetery wall," he would tease.

"No you can't," they would protest, laughing at the picture of him leaping over the wall.

"Yes, I can!" he'd respond and the fun would begin.

In and out they would run – round the garden, in through the French doors, into the kitchen, down into the basement, along the hallways, up and down the stairs.

"You can't catch me," they would yell, but of course he always did. They were sad to see this happy, energetic young uncle leave to return to the horrors of the war.

Even in the midst of the Blitz, Christmas was a time to be enjoyed. Apart from the usual excitement of school holidays and presents on Christmas Day, Harold and Pat looked forward to going carol-singing – not only because they enjoyed singing but also for a rather more lucrative reason! They always made sure that one of the houses visited was the home of a local headmaster and his wife. Their home, on an avenue that ran up the side of the Hilly Fields, was called 'St David's' so, naturally enough, one particular carol was always on the songlist – 'Once in Royal David's City' – how subtle!

The couple loved to see them coming and would usher them into the living room where they would sing their hearts out – like little Tommy Tucker, singing for his supper. The headmaster's wife always gave them a big homemade biscuit, a hot juicy drink and a half crown. Their earnings meant that Harold and Pat could go to the large Hippodrome to see the Pantomime – a very exciting occasion.

Others in London didn't always share the children's enjoyment of life. Behind the college on top of the Hilly Fields, some Nisson huts had been erected for young ATS girls. Somehow, as children often do, Harold and Pat made friends with them and introduced their Mother to them during a walk in the Park. May felt sorry for them and invited them over to her house for a cup of tea. About eight young girls went, all in need of a little tender, loving care. They were finding it difficult coping with the war and being away from home. May cheered them up and they became very fond of her.

One evening, May opened up the two large rooms into one and the young ladies brought their friends. They played records on the gramophone and soon were singing along to the music. One or two had a wee weep, as they thought longingly of home and family. One girl wanted to acknowledge May's warm hospitality and gave her a ring she was wearing. May protested but the girl insisted, so grateful was she for this wonderful light relief from the tensions of the war. Of course May understood how they all felt as she herself was homesick for Ireland. Little did she know that her homesickness may well have been the first little step in God's greater plan, to give to her daughter a passionate love for Ireland and a passionate desire to see God's Kingdom come to that land.

## Chapter 4
# Difficult Days

IN 1942, A baby brother arrived for Harold and Pat. He was a gentle child with a placid nature and Joseph and May decided to name him Joseph, in memory of the little boy they had lost. He too had been blessed with a lovely nature.

At this stage in the war, Pat's father had been put into the Military Police and his job included escorting German prisoners to and from their cells. Some of them used to ask Joseph about his family and one day, as he was about to go on leave, they presented him with three gifts for the children – an aeroplane for Harold, a doll's cradle for Pat and a table tennis bat for Joey which had four birds on top and strings below with a weight on. When the bat was lifted up and down, the birds would peck the bat with their beaks. All three toys were made out of wood carved by a penknife. The windows on the plane, the eyes of the birds and the motifs on the cradle were done with a burnt match – what skill that required! It was a wonderful example of the many little kindnesses shown by an enemy that stood in sharp contrast to the brutality that was more usually displayed in those years. The children were delighted with the gifts, despite the fact that Pat had no doll to put in her cradle and money was too scarce to buy one.

Towards the end of the war, May became ill and her illness resulted in some very difficult days for the children. On numerous occasions May would feel a great well of pain in her abdomen, often causing her to collapse on the floor or to drop trays of dishes. She visited five different doctors to find some explanation for the pain but all of them gave the same diagnosis – it was all in her mind!

Fortunately a Christian lady called Mrs Fennel, who used to visit from time to time, happened to say to her after one of these episodes,

"My dear, there's a lady doctor who lives in Chudleigh Avenue, not far from you. She's very clever – from your own home country, from Belfast. She studied at Queen's University. If anyone can help you, she can!"

Doctor Dunlop duly called at the home and immediately sent for an ambulance which carried May off to see Sir John Peel, the Queen's specialist, no less! Even this famous physician couldn't make a diagnosis so Dr Dunlop passed on her own diagnosis – an ectopic pregnancy. May was operated on immediately as this was a life-threatening condition. Pat's Mum had not even been aware that she was pregnant!

May's convalescence meant another separation for the family. It was arranged for Harold and Pat to go to an American nursery in North London while baby Joe was sent to another nursery in Devon, a couple of hundred miles away.

After Pat's previous experience of evacuation, this new move was traumatic. She was so frightened that she wet the bed in the girls' bedroom on the first night. It was a large room which held about seven beds. The floor was highly polished and the beds were high hospital beds so everyone could hear and see Pat's plight – such a humiliating experience for a little girl, just about five years old. The other children 'oohed' and 'aahed' at her disgrace and she felt ashamed.

She settled in eventually and even discovered that this new situation had some compensations. One of these was the park which ran along the back of the big house. At the bottom of the long garden was a wooden humped-back bridge over a stream which led into a wood – an exciting playground for Harold and Pat. The autumn leaves rustled under their feet and fallen twiglets from the trees cracked when they stepped on them. Acorns and fir cones were everywhere – a great treasure trove. If they were very quiet, they would catch a glimpse of the busy squirrels as they darted up and down and around the trees.

The other compensation was a weekly visit to the local cinema, under the supervision of one of the nursery attendants. Not even the scolding from Matron for annoying the other girls by singing the film songs before she went to sleep could dampen Pat's joy in these outings! In later years, she would remember the Nursery with great affection and the sight of a dark green door with stained-glass windows would make her heart leap with tender memories of the days she spent behind a similar door.

Poor little Joey didn't fare so well. Despite being only eighteen months old, the horror of being plunged into a bath of extremely hot water, lifted up by his hair and scrubbed all over with a huge scrubbing brush, was seared into his memory, never to be forgotten. He was too young to tell them what had happened to him but they could see that he had been ill-treated – he was thin and frightened. May tried one day to find out what he had been through and simply said,

"Here comes the Matron!"

Joey's reaction was instant and alarming. He couldn't walk or talk but on hearing those words, he shuffled across the kitchen to hide under the table, his little face white as chalk and his heart pounding. It took May a long time to comfort him and stop him shaking.

Pat's difficult days were rather different but nonetheless distressing for a little girl. Pat was about six years old when a new pupil joined her class and was told to share Pat's desk. There were two things that fascinated Pat at that time – ladies' red high-heeled shoes and rings. The new pupil, whose name was Ivy, pestered Pat all that first day to go home with her to her house after school.

"No I can't," Pat said time after time, "my Mum doesn't allow me."

"Look," said Ivy, holding out her hand, "if you come with me, I'll give you that ring."

Pat looked at the ring and could resist no longer, so the two girls set out after school to Ivy's house, about a mile from the school in the opposite direction to Pat's house. Pat was persuaded to tell Ivy's Mum that she had permission from her own Mum and the two girls had a great time playing, hardly noticing the time passing.

It was ten o'clock before she left and only then did the enormity of what she had done finally hit her – it was dark by the time she reached the main road and she felt very lost. Tears were streaming down her face as she hurried to where she hoped her home was.

Meanwhile, May got more and more frantic when Pat didn't return home from school. She searched up and down the road repeatedly, then finally, in desperation, she got on a bus and headed for Lewisham, watching anxiously all along the road. Miraculously, she caught a glimpse of the now sobbing Pat and called to the conductor to let her off the bus.

When May heard Pat's story, she was extremely annoyed and marched back to Ivy's house, to return the ring and to make it clear how upset she was.

"That's one little tinker," said Ivy's Mum. "Ivy!" she called.

There was no response to her shout and she went to investigate.

"She's under the table," she informed May, "I'll give her a good smacking."

Somehow May didn't think that would ever happen so next day, she sent Pat to school with a letter telling the teacher about Ivy's poor influence on her and asking her to keep a watchful eye. The note was handed on to the Headmistress and after Assembly, to Pat's utter bewilderment, she was not allowed to go back to class but was made to stand on a stool with her face to the wall for the whole morning. When Harold went home at lunch time without Pat, May was furious and set off for the school.

She arrived at the Assembly Hall to find Pat still standing on the stool and discovered, when she lifted her down, that Pat had wet herself in her distress.

"How dare you do this to my daughter!" she stormed angrily at the Headmistress. She could hardly take it in when Miss Halsie sat very calmly at her desk and offered no other explanation for her behaviour than the fact that she hated the Irish! Pat and Harold were very promptly removed from the school and didn't return until Miss Halsie left and was replaced by another headmistress.

After Joey's birth, three more children arrived, Valerie, Roy and Noel. Although each new birth was greeted with great joy by the household, it also meant increased work and responsibility for the two older children. May's health was not very good – at one time she was so depressed that she didn't go out for two years – so for a long time, Harold was the one who really kept the family going. He collected the Family Allowance and did the shopping and the cooking, while Pat looked after the house. Harold also had to leave Valerie to her nursery school and often arrived late at his own school. This would result in the inevitable caning from his teacher and invariably he would collapse on to the Assembly Hall floor. Despite the unfairness of the situation, he never breathed a word to his mother in case it upset her. Difficult days indeed!

But even in the midst of hard times, Pat saw God's hand on her family in miraculous ways. At the time of Roy's birth, she became worried enough about her mother to phone a doctor. She was told later that if they had been left for another hour, both May and Roy would have died. Pat was learning, even in childhood, how to hear and obey God's Voice in her ear – wonderful preparation for being His handmaiden.

Another example of God's hand of protection occurred after Noel's birth. May was ill after the birth and stayed in her bedroom for some days. When she decided she was well enough to get up, Pat set to work. She washed the children and the babies, lit the fire, set the table nicely in the kitchen and put Noel in his pram beside the fire – all ready to serve breakfast, exhausted by her efforts but happy to have everything "just right" for her Mum. Much to Pat's disappointment, May walked into the kitchen and said,

"Oh you've lit the fire in the kitchen. I would like to go into the family room. I'll light the fire and you bring the breakfast things through."

Just as Joe and Pat were wheeling Noel's pram out of the kitchen, the ceiling collapsed above where the pram had been, raining down plaster and dust. What a shock! What a narrow escape!

Her little sister, Valerie, was also saved from near death when she was about four years old. Pat was chatting to a neighbour's daughter and keeping an eye on Valerie. Suddenly the little girl dashed out on to the road. To Pat's horror, she saw a double decker bus speeding round the bend. She sat frozen to the spot, unable to shout or scream a warning, while the driver slammed on his brakes and only just managed to stop the bus before it reached the little girl. Valerie seemed unaware of the danger she was in and just danced back on to the pavement.

In later years, over all of these incidents, Pat would see the good hand of her God in the life of her family and would rejoice at His power and protection.

Chapter 5
# The Voice in the Laburnum Tree

THE NEVER-ENDING hard work and immense responsibility in helping to run the family home finally took its toll on Pat and she herself became ill and depressed. Thankfully May seemed to have some appreciation of what was happening and sent Pat off on her first ever holiday to her Uncle Billy and Aunt Betty in Scotland.

The journey from London to Glasgow was long – Pat left at six o'clock in the morning and didn't arrive until midnight, tired, anxious and tearful because she wasn't sure exactly where to get off the bus. Despite this rather uncertain start, Pat had a wonderful time in Glasgow with her cousin, William, and some other children whom her aunt knew. They played bowls in Alexandra Park and rowed a boat on Huggins Field Lough. It was as though, for the first time in her life, she could just be a child – carefree and happy. She acquired a new confidence as well as a new Scottish accent! On her return to school, the girls used to ask her to tell them about her holiday, just to hear "the funny way" she spoke.

Illness was never far away – at the age of twelve, she had threatened meningitis and the doctor ordered complete bed rest. Pat spent the time drawing and designing dresses, coats and suits. A local schoolteacher collected the designs three times a week, made the clothes and sold them. Pat's early career as a fashion designer didn't make her rich – she never thought that she might be entitled to a share in the profits!

A feeling of depression continued to shadow Pat right through teenage years but a real turning point happened for her one glorious sunny day. Despite the beautiful day, Pat felt dark and depressed inside and thought she would climb out on to the verandah to try and cheer herself up. As she sat alone with her dark thoughts, she could hear her Mum chatting to Mrs Fennel in the room below – they had opened the French doors to take advantage of the beautiful day. Somehow the fact that they were enjoying themselves just annoyed Pat.

"How can they just sit there chatting for hours when I feel so bad?" she thought, somewhat irrationally.

She started to cry – great agonising sobs. Now and again, in between her sobs, she could hear her Mum say,

"I wonder where Patsy is?"

"If she really cared, she would come and look for me – she would know how I'm feeling," Pat would think and the feeling would well up once more.

Between the heat of the day and the exertion of crying, Pat was left exhausted but still couldn't stop herself crying. Suddenly she heard a Voice saying to her,

"Look up into the Laburnum tree."

She never even wondered who had spoken, just did as the Voice asked. She looked up into the beautiful, hundred year old tree, dressed for summer in its yellow blooms and followed the line of its branches into the garden below. Such beauty calmed her soul and dried her tears. She was conscious of being bathed in a wonderful sense of peace. She sat there for a long time, just basking in the peace. Pat didn't know whose Voice she had heard and didn't understand the peace she was experiencing but was grateful for it.

It would be some years before it would dawn on her that the Voice was Jesus' voice, the One who promises "a peace that passes understanding", but a year or two later she did experience the peace again. A Presbyterian minister's daughter, Eunice, whose family lived above Pat's home, invited Pat and her friend, Barbara, to go to a meeting in Lewisham. They agreed to go – it was something to do, after all.

The home to which they were taken was a very dark, ancient house, full of beautiful polished furniture and wooden banisters. The young girls were hurried to a small, candle-lit room at the top of the house, where a number of other young people had gathered. A very old gentleman spoke to them and at the end made an appeal for a show of hands to indicate those who would like to go to another room to hear more. Barbara and Pat both raised their hands and were led up three steps to an even tinier room. Pat felt a bit like Alice-in-Wonderland at this stage! The old gentleman talked to them and prayed with them and as he did so, Pat knew once again the peace she had experienced before. It would be difficult to assess if this was a 'conversion' experience or not but it was certainly a little step along Pat's faith journey, another obedient response to His Voice.

## Chapter 6
# A New Life

PAT HEARD THE Voice again, when she was fifteen, just after she had left school. She wasn't sure what to do about her future and May was keen for her just to stay at home and not go to work. There would always be enough to keep her busy, helping with the other children.

This wasn't part of God's plan for her life and one day when she was hanging out the babies' clothes on the washing line, she clearly heard the Voice again, saying,

"Put on your red suit and go and see your employment officer."

Pat did as the Voice suggested – washed and curled her hair and put on her red suit, then set off to see her employment officer who sent her for an interview to train in Window Dressing, a profession that was eagerly sought after by many young people. Pat had no idea that a certificate she had received while still at school for her artistic efforts in sculpting a lady's head, would be the very thing that would give her access to training for the top qualification.

On her final day at school, she had been allowed to work with leftover clay and to her teacher's amazement, had shaped the head in about ten minutes, using no tools, only her hands. The teacher had brought the Headmaster to see it and he too had been amazed. He had taken it, baked it and kept it in his study. Pat had known a great sense of excitement and fulfilment in sculpting the head and in later years even wondered if she might have made a career of it. God had other plans for her life and used the certificate to begin to place her on His path.

The nephew of the founders of C&A Modes brought her into a large office. He was a pleasant man who soon put her at ease with his initial questions.

"I can see that you have considerable artistic talent," he said with a smile, "and I'm very impressed that you have come to the interview on your own."

Pat thought wryly that she didn't really have much choice!

"Do you have a black dress?" was his next question.

Pat replied rather fearfully,

"No, I only have a green one."

Her interviewer didn't seem to be unduly concerned by her lack of suitable clothing, just smiled and said,

"Can you start on Monday morning?"

As Pat made her way home, she found it hard to believe that she had managed to acquire a job as easily as she had but didn't fully realise how unusual her position was until she turned up for work the following Monday.

"How did you manage to get that job?" one after another asked her as they introduced themselves to her in the canteen.

"I've been in a queue for a similar job for over a year now," added one girl. Pat discovered that it was very unusual for someone to be given the training for window dressing without first spending a considerable length of time on the shop floor.

She was well trained at C&A, spending the next eighteen months travelling round their various branches, getting experience in displaying different types of clothing in their extensive shop windows. She discovered that many of the high class shops only trained their window dressers in one type of clothing – shoes, coats, millinery or dresses – but she had been trained in them all. It was, of course, all part of God's great plan for His handmaiden because her range of experience brought her to the attention of the bosses at Head Office and she was summoned to an interview with one of them who had travelled from Head Office to Lewisham to talk to her.

"I understand your Mother is Irish," were his opening words.

"Yes, that's right," said Pat, wondering what was coming next.

"We're opening a new branch of C&A Modes soon, in Belfast, and we'd like you to be the head girl of Display there, responsible for training other girls. This would mean a raise in pay, of course," he added as an extra incentive.

Pat didn't really need any added incentive for she had always been curious about May's homeland and the chance to see Ireland for herself was too good to miss.

May and Joseph began planning for Pat to stay with her Aunt Emily and family who lived on the Ormeau Road but once again they began to see God at work, doing "exceedingly abundantly above all that we ask or seek". At the same time as this was happening in Pat's life, May's doctors and social worker became very concerned about the long term homesickness that was contributing to her ongoing depression. They offered to see what they could do to help and to the family's surprise, a letter arrived informing them that a four-bedroomed house was available for them in Carrickfergus, if May could confirm that she had a relative born in that area. She was able to confirm that her father had been born near there and to her absolute delight, the reply came to say that the house was theirs if Joseph would travel to Carrickfergus and choose which one he wanted. What a wonderful example of God's perfect timing!

Joseph left for Ireland as quickly as possible and the excited family packed up their home in London. Joseph could hardly contain his joy when he returned.

"May," he said, "you should see it! It's a beautiful town. I stood on a bridge and took these photos."

As he spoke, he pointed to one of the photos – in it was a beautiful old red brick house with the Belfast Lough flowing below it. May learnt later that this particular house belonged to one of her relatives.

Moving home always means saying goodbye and so May made arrangements for them to spend a day with her brother Tommy and his wife Eileen in Farnborough. Their house was right beside the airfield and Uncle Tom entertained the children with tales of exciting things that had happened there. They met their cousins Tom, Lorna and Joyce and really enjoyed their time with them and felt quite sad when they had to leave.

They also had to say goodbye to Harold who had been called up by the Airforce to do his National Service. Having been born in Ireland, it wasn't compulsory for him to go, but he was rather excited by the prospect of the eight weeks' training he would receive. So there were hugs, kisses and a few tears all round as Harold set off and then the rest of the family made their way to Scotland, where May and the other children would have to wait until the container carrying their belongings arrived in Northern Ireland.

They all enjoyed the journey through the beautiful mountains of the Lake District and on in to Scotland and Pat was overjoyed to be reunited with her Uncle Billy, Aunt Betty and cousin William, whom she remembered with great affection. What a warm welcome they received in that cosy home, how they laughed at their fun-loving Uncle Billy and how they appreciated the aroma of the bread each morning, fresh from the nearby bakery. Pat almost didn't want to leave this place where she had been so happy but soon it was time to move on to the next part of God's plan for her life.

## Chapter 7
# Settling In

JOSEPH AND PAT stood in the bright sunshine on the deck of the huge ferry, as it made its way slowly into Belfast Lough. Pat had rarely seen her father so excited – he was a man of few words!

"Oh isn't that just beautiful," Pat called to him, as she caught sight of a high cliff and the greenest grass she had ever seen on the slope at the top. She would never forget this first view of Ireland and, as the ferry chugged along past ever more beautiful scenery, she began to understand why her mother felt as she did about this country.

"Look!" called Joseph, "that's Carrickfergus Castle! That's where we're going to live."

"What an amazing place," thought Pat, "imagine living so close to a castle like that – nine hundred years old!"

She took a deep breath and filled her lungs with the clean fresh air, so different to the heavily polluted air in London. As she watched the ship docking, she was filled with joy at the thought of living on this beautiful island but also some trepidation as she contemplated her new job in Belfast.

Pat and her father caught a bus to the Ormeau Road, where Joseph and all his brothers and sisters had been born. Pat was introduced to her Aunt Martha, Uncle Jack and two more new cousins - Marlene and Joanie.

"Come on in and have a wee cup of tea," they were urged and Pat sat watching in astonishment as a round polished table was set up, a white linen cloth was slid into place, fine china and good cutlery were arranged and finally a sumptuous array of homebaking was carefully set down in the middle.

"She said she was only going to make a cup of tea!" Pat whispered to her father.

"Ah girl," he replied in a light hearted tone that revealed his joy at being back home, "none of your English cups of tea here with nothing to eat – you're in Ireland now!"

Many years later Pat would discover that her Uncle Jack's nephew was destined to become a well-known preacher in Northern Ireland – Hedley Murphy. Pat had the pleasure of hearing him speak when she attended a gospel meeting. Unfortunately her Uncle didn't know his nephew's Saviour, though his family worshipped at a local Gospel Hall.

Later that day, they walked to Knockbreda, where they had arranged to stay with Pat's Aunt Emily, Uncle Bertie and some more cousins – David, Yvonne, Brian, Helen and Barbara. The next day, Uncle Bertie drove Joseph to Carrickfergus, so that he could sign for the house and pick up the keys.

Once a cooker had been installed in the house, Pat and Joseph made the journey to their new home on a double decker bus. Pat enjoyed the wonderful views all the way along the Lough shore. They went into the town, bought two sets of cutlery, plates, cups and groceries for an Ulster Fry. Pat had never tasted an Ulster Fry and so Joseph was the chief cook for their first meal in their new home. They had no furniture so they sat on the stairs to eat it. Pat would never forget her first introduction to this culinary delight, especially the fried soda bread, cooked to just the right golden brown colour.

Meanwhile, Pat had begun to settle into her new position with C&A Modes. People in the city were excited by this new trendy shop where they could buy fashionable clothes much more cheaply than in the other large fashion houses in Belfast. Pat enjoyed displaying the clothes to their best advantage and training those on her team how to do so too. She even got the chance to do some modelling of the clothes - the photographs were taken in front of the City Hall. A professional model was brought in to teach the girls how to walk and pose for the cameras and Pat was paid with a cream coat - no exorbitant modelling fees for these models!

May and the rest of the family arrived in August and Joseph and Pat went to Carrick Station to meet them. When May used to talk to the children about Ireland, she would always say,

"When I arrive in Ireland, the bands will come and meet me."

Sure enough, as Joseph and Pat stood on the station steps and May walked out from the station, the town was full of bands and some were even playing right outside the station. The look on May's face was priceless! Unknown to her, the date of her arrival was the last Saturday in August, one of the dates when the bands all marched in processions all over Northern Ireland. That particular year, it had been the turn of Carrickfergus to host the bands in that area. Pat often laughed when she remembered that day and it all helped to confirm her opinion that her God had a sense of humour!

Once they had settled into their new home, their cousins Marlene and Joanie would often come to stay with them in the summer holidays and Pat discovered that her brother Harold had a good sense of humour too. He loved to play tricks on the unsuspecting little girls and they didn't seem to mind being on the receiving end. On one occasion, he brought out a dinner plate and carefully held it up against the ceiling of the living room. He said nothing and Marlene and Joanie soon started trying to find out what he was doing. He pretended not to hear their questions at first, then he turned to Marlene and said,

"Marlene, you would be the right height. Could you go and fetch the broom from the broom cupboard?"

Marlene did as requested and Harold instructed her,

"Very carefully now – place the handle end right in the centre of the plate."

Again she did as she was told. Harold then sat down in the armchair and started to read the newspaper. Too late, Marlene realised that she had been tricked and she began to laugh and shouted out,

"You've tricked me!"

The next few minutes provided great amusement for everyone - the more Marlene laughed the more the plate slid along the ceiling and the more desperate her efforts to save it from falling. Harold took pity on her eventually and lifted the plate down.

He managed to catch Joanie out as well a couple of years later. Harold took off his jacket and began examining the sleeve, looking all over it and looking inside it.

"Boy, there's something desperately wrong on the inside of this sleeve. Every time I wear it, I find it most annoying. Here, Joanie, the sun's shining brightly – could you sit in that chair by the window and catch the light through the cuff of the sleeve as I hold the jacket up high. Then we can look in both ends and maybe we'll see what's wrong with it."

Joanie moved over to the chair and did as she was told. They both started smiling because they could see each other down the sleeve.

"Ah," said Harold, "now I can see the problem, Can you see it?"

"No," replied Joanie, not very sure just what she was supposed to be looking for!

"Look – I know," went on her tormentor, "Keep looking and you'll soon see the problem."

With that, he lifted a small jug of water he'd hidden earlier and proceeded to pour it down the sleeve into her laughing face. She squealed, let go of the sleeve and ran to dry her face, then chased him round the garden with the towel. The two girls just loved him, in much the same way that Pat and Harold had loved their Uncle Dick.

## Chapter 8
# Choosing Christ

ALTHOUGH PAT'S FATHER was from a Church of Ireland background, she and her mother began attending the local Gospel Hall on Sunday evenings and also went to the mid-week Bible study, which was held in a house beside the Hall. At one of the Bible Study meetings, during the singing of a hymn, Pat had a strong sense that God was speaking to her about her need of salvation. She thought about it all the way home and once there, knelt at the side of her bed to ask Christ to come into her heart and to forgive her sins. She then very simply trusted in His mercy and His promise to save her.

It was obvious when she arrived in work the next day that something had happened – the usually well-made-up face was devoid of make-up! Before she even had a chance to share her wonderful news with the girls, her boss's assistant, who quickly realised what had transpired when he saw Pat's pale face, began to tease and mock her about being saved.

Besides putting up with teasing from her colleagues, Pat faced the uncomfortable task of telling her new boyfriend about the commitment she had made. She had been dating George for a short time and he had just told her the plans he had made for the 11th and 12th July.

"We'll go to my home first so that you can meet my parents," he said excitedly, "and then we'll row across the river in a little boat to the Hop. I'll introduce you to some of my other friends from Campbell College."

Pat had been looking forward to what promised to be a very romantic evening but knew that she had to be honest with George. He wasn't too pleased to hear her news but agreed that they would take a break for a week so that he could decide if he would become a Christian too. He called to see her at the end of the week but he felt the commitment was too much for him and so they went their separate ways.

Strangely enough, the ending of the relationship didn't perturb Pat as much as it might have because she had chosen Christ and was supremely happy in her relationship with Him. She began to attend the Saturday night Christian rallies, the Rendezvous, in Grosvenor Hall. When she sang God's praise in these huge gatherings of young people, her heart would swell with joy and she revelled in the fun and fellowship afterwards in the popular café, Chalet D'Or.

Pat also discovered the wonder of personal intimacy with God and just loved to lie on top of the bed in her tiny bedroom and commune with God. He became more real to her than anyone on earth. Her Mum eventually became anxious because she often went to her room at eight o'clock in the evening and didn't appear downstairs for the rest of the night. May felt this was unnatural behaviour for a young woman.

"You should go out more – enjoy yourself," she would urge. When Pat didn't seem too keen on that idea she would try to prise her out of the bedroom in another way.

"You don't even come and sit with us in the evening," she would scold, "It's not good to be on your own all the time."

For the first six months all went well. Pat continued to attend the Gospel Hall and was befriended by the Logan family and others in the Assembly, who often invited her to supper. While she enjoyed meeting the various people, she began to find that some of the things that were happening had little to do with God and the fellowship she found there never measured up to the rich intimacy she knew was possible. She lost heart and stopped going. Soon she had stopped going to church altogether and thought of those who did as hypocrites.

Pat had never really been told about spiritual growth and knew nothing at all about the great battle into which she had been thrust. She had never heard of Satan who saw the potential in this young girl and was determined to erode her faith. It wasn't in his interests that she should serve the Great God as His handmaiden and he used her friends and her lack of teaching to spoil the special new relationship with God that she had been enjoying.

Although Pat was no longer close to God, He continued to work out His plan for her life and part of that plan included a young man called Hugh Logan. One Saturday morning, Hugh and his friend happened to meet in Belfast and stopped to chat outside the C&A shop window, when they caught sight of Pat and one of the other window dressers, called Nessa, busy replacing the garments that had been sold from the window. Nessa, as usual, looked wonderful and smiled at the young men on the other side of the window but Pat felt pale and unattractive and did her best to hide behind one of the fixtures. Hugh's friend noticed Nessa and remarked to Hugh,

"There's a lovely girl!"

Hugh had caught sight of Pat and replied,

"There's a far nicer wee girl there."

He smiled at Pat and she blushed bright red. He remembered seeing Pat before – in Portrush the previous Easter. Hugh was the trumpeter in a band called The White Eagles. That Easter they had been following in the footsteps of one of Ireland's top bands, the Dave Glover Band, playing on the green slope of grass at the front of the Arcadia. Pat had often caught sight of them speeding all over the town in a friend's sports car. So when Nessa coaxed Pat to go to a dance at which Hugh was playing, Pat succumbed to temptation, even though at that time she had no desire to go away from God. She so enjoyed the foot-tapping jazz and blues songs played by the band and especially loved the hymns they played in their own special arrangements – "Precious Lord, Take my Hand" and "Just a Closer Walk with Thee". The enemy certainly knew which button to press to pull her away from her deep communion with God. She was caught up in a whirl of wonderful tunes and fancy dance steps.

Some of Nessa's friends left her home afterwards but the conversation in the car was almost non-existent and Pat asked to be dropped off in the middle of Carrickfergus.

"Now what did I do that for?" she asked herself ruefully, as she quickly realised just what the one-and-a-half mile walk home was going to be like. The wind and storm howled around her and she pulled her fashionably huge collar up as high as she could around her head to provide some protection. She struggled along in her very high stiletto shoes, keeping as close as possible to the shops and buildings on the side of the road furthest away from the sea. Even so, the fierce winds at times dragged her out into the road towards the sea wall. It was fortunate that there was a shortage of petrol at that time and there were fewer cars than usual on the road. Otherwise her life might well have been in danger – it was a stormy end to a wonderful evening!

Some months later, Pat met Hugh again at a dance in Queen's University, where his band was playing. She missed her last bus home and Hugh offered her a lift in his Dad's car. As the car drew up outside Pat's home, she opened her purse to give him money towards the petrol. Hugh just laughed,

"What about a goodnight kiss instead? And would you be free to come to the Ritz Cinema next Thursday night?"

Pat was surprised but leaned across to give him a faltering peck on the cheek and muttered quickly,

"Goodnight – see you next Thursday."

And so began a routine of going out together every Tuesday, Thursday and Saturday night. The band travelled to their gigs in a Morris Minor, which presented a bit of a problem as one of their instruments was a double bass! The problem was solved by opening the window and letting the huge instrument travel half in and half out of the car. Getting Pat into the venues was another little problem they faced –

"Say you're the singer," she was urged the first few times she travelled with them but then she appeared so often that they began to say,

"You'll just have to do some singing to earn your keep!"

Although neither Hugh nor Pat would have considered themselves to be committed Christians at this point, the odd thing was that their private conversations often turned to the Lord and Salvation. Hugh was rather puzzled by Pat and would sometimes quiz her -

"You say you're saved?" he would ask.

"Yes," she would reply but even as she did, her heart would rebuke her.

"Then if you say you're saved, why are you going to dances?"

Pat knew that her behaviour at that time wasn't consistent with what was considered to be Christian behaviour and so she had no answer for him. God was using Hugh to remind His handmaiden that He still had His hand on her.

## Chapter 9
# Wedding Bells

EVENTUALLY THE RELATIONSHIP with Hugh became serious enough for him to bring her home to meet his parents. At this stage, she knew almost nothing about Hugh's family or background, only that he lived in Ballynure, a small country village not far from Carrickfergus. To Pat's surprise, instead of leading her to one of the humbler homes which stood in a row in the village, Hugh opened the gate to a large farmhouse. His mother, a warm, friendly woman, welcomed her at the front door and brought them into the dining room, where a warm fire glowed.

As Pat sipped her afternoon tea, she looked up at Hugh who was standing in front of the fire, dressed in his green corduroy jacket and brown suede shoes. He sported a black beard in those days and Pat thought that he looked every inch the Lord of the Manor – he seemed to suit the fine old house. She met his father and his brothers, David and Brian, as well as his two maiden aunts, Daisy and Margaret. Daisy was a talented oil painter, sang in the Ballynure Methodist Choir and was a Sunday School teacher. Margaret was also a Sunday School teacher, played the organ and had been a governess in England to several Lords' and Ladies' children.

"Let's go outside," said Hugh when they had finished their tea, "I'd like to show you the fields at the back of the house."

It was a sunny spring day and Pat was entranced by the primroses that seemed to be growing everywhere. She wasn't just so happy about the cows in the fields – it was the first time she had ever been close to cows and she was a bit dismayed to discover that they were very curious animals and kept edging closer and closer to her. She was even less happy when she trod in some cows' manure! Hugh, however, managed to brighten her day – he led her to a stream, set her down on a boulder, then knelt to remove her shoe. He proceeded to wash it in the river and then knelt again, like Prince Charming of old, to put it back on her foot. He then capped it all by picking a posy of primroses for her – a truly romantic gesture!

On their return, Hugh and his brothers played cricket while Pat helped to make the tea. This was just the first of many visits to the family home at Ballynure. It was a quaint place – part of its charm was that it didn't seem to have moved into the twentieth century and had retained a pace of life and an air of refinement from a former time. Pat enjoyed the wonderful meals cooked by Hugh's mother and got to know and love his family.

It was no surprise to anyone when Hugh and Pat decided to get engaged on her twenty-first birthday, in March, 1959. There was no formal proposal, just a growing awareness that they were meant for each other. They celebrated simply - on the day of their engagement, Hugh met Pat after work and they went for a meal to a rather posh restaurant near C&A. The meal was lovely and Pat enjoyed every minute of it, despite feeling nervous at eating in more formal surroundings that she was used to. As they came to the last course of coffee or tea and cheese and biscuits, the waiter stood at their table, napkin over his arm and enquired,

"Shall I pour now, Madam?"

Pat was so nervous she didn't hear him properly and thought he had said,

"Port and lemon, Madam?"

She thought they were being offered a celebratory drink on the house and in her best polite voice, replied,

"No thank you, I don't drink."

The quizzical looks on the faces of both Hugh and the waiter told her that she had said the wrong thing. Hugh soon put her right and the waiter proceeded to pour the tea and coffee. They could hardly drink it for laughing!

The more Pat thought about her engagement in the days that followed, the more she came to realise that she wanted more than just a meal to remember it by and she said to Hugh one day,

"Hugh, I'd love to go and ask God's blessing on our engagement."

Although he was rather surprised at her request, he agreed that it would be a good thing to do and so the first Saturday that Pat was off work, they made their way to Ballynure Methodist Church, having borrowed the key from Hugh's Aunt Margaret. It was a warm day and the sun was shining brightly outside but inside the church it was beautifully cool. There was no one else in the building but they sensed the Presence of God Himself as they walked up to the Altar and knelt before Him. In the peaceful atmosphere of the little church, they held hands and very simply asked God to bless their engagement and to keep them together for always. They had no idea, as they knelt in the silence, just how significant that request was and how Satan would do his best to destroy their relationship.

One of the girls in the band was also engaged and she and her fiancé had a rather volatile relationship. She would often say to Pat,

"Teddy and I had a row and I just threw the ring at him!"

Pat began to feel that she was letting Hugh get off very lightly so the next time they had a disagreement, she threw her ring at him too! She soon realised what a very bad idea that had been! She was heartbroken and cried her eyes out in the privacy of her room. She missed him so much.

"Why did I do a stupid thing like that?" she berated herself. "What was I thinking about?"

It was October before they got back together again and almost as soon as they did Hugh said,

"Look, let's get married. I'm tired of all this to-ing and fro-ing."

Pat agreed and they worked out that the earliest they could get married was January 16th , just three months away. They visited their respective parents to tell them their exciting news and were rather taken aback when the reaction they got wasn't quite what they had anticipated.

"That's very soon," they both said and Pat and Hugh soon realised that hanging in the air was an unspoken question,

"Could there be a baby on the way?"

Once they were assured that this was not to be a shotgun wedding, they were happy and Hugh's Mum even agreed to make the three-tier wedding cake. The necessary arrangements were made – Knock Methodist was booked for the service and the Park Avenue Hotel was booked for the reception. Invitations were sent out to sixty guests. Bridesmaids and a best man were chosen. Hugh's brother, Dave accepted his role as best man and Pat's sixteen year old friend, Nancy Martin, and her twelve year old sister, Valerie, were delighted to be asked to act as bridesmaids and enjoyed helping to choose their blue satin dresses and matching shoes.

Soon everything was in place and all they had to worry about was the weather – there had been some heavy snowfalls in the days leading up to the Big Day but the 16th January dawned bright and sunny – more like a day in Spring than in the middle of Winter. The day didn't begin too well – Pat's mother wasn't feeling well so it was left to the bride to get everyone ready. She rushed around making breakfast and checking that her younger brothers, Roy and Noel were properly washed and dressed. Then Valerie had to be helped into her bridesmaid's dress and Pat had to do her mother's make-up. The older bridesmaid didn't arrive until it was almost time to go so Pat was glad that her neighbour had come in earlier to wash her hair and apply a face mask. She was left with just ten minutes to put on her white French lace wedding gown and apply her own make-up.

In the middle of all the panic, the postman arrived.

"There's a letter for you, Pat," someone shouted and she hurried over to get it, thinking that she had enough to do without having to read letters as well! She recognised Hugh's writing on the envelope and for a fleeting moment was scared to open it.

"What if he has had second thoughts?" she wondered as she slit the top of the envelope. She needn't have worried for the letter was a most welcome love letter, perfectly timed to arrive on the wedding morning. The love expressed in its lines more than made up for the pressures of "getting to the church on time".

The wedding car arrived, Pat and her father were driven to the church and as they began their slow procession up the aisle, her father whispered in her ear,

"It's alright – he's there!"

Pat's face broke into a wide smile as she caught sight of Hugh and the smile never left her face for the rest of the day. Only one thing spoilt the perfection of the occasion – Harold had arranged to go to the church with their next door neighbours but unfortunately, their car broke down and he missed the entire marriage service, just arriving in time to be included in the photographs.

The day flew past and all too soon it was time to leave for their honeymoon. They had quite a rush to catch the four o'clock train for Dublin but made it in time and settled back in their seats for the long journey. Pat noticed that people who met them on the train kept smiling at them and she couldn't understand at first why they were being so friendly until she realised that their newly married status was plain for all to see – there were tell-tale bits of confetti caught up in the veil of her hat!

So the next part of the Lord's plan for His handmaiden was fulfilled – to provide her with a partner in life who would love her and support her and for whom God had great purposes too. His handmaiden, of course, was unaware of all of this – she was too busy getting used to the idea of being Mrs Logan!

## Chapter 10
# Break Up

"HELLO, MRS LOGAN!" the young boy yelled as he flew past Pat on his bicycle. Pat recognised him as her neighbour's son and opened her mouth to reply to him.

"Oh no, he's not speaking to me, he said 'Mrs Logan'," she thought and then began to laugh at herself.

"Silly me – it was me he was shouting at – I am Mrs Logan!"

Even after a week of married life it still took a bit of getting used to – a new name, a new husband and a new place to live. Their home for the first six months was a private hotel on the Cliftonville Road. They had decided to rent a few rooms in it while a new bungalow was being built for them at Glengormley. The site for the new house was high up in the hills above Belfast and Pat looked forward to the breathtaking views she would enjoy when she eventually moved in. She was to discover that wonderful views often come at a price and the price in this case was the trek up a steep hill that had to be negotiated each evening after work. The bus from her work didn't go as far as her road so she had no alternative but to walk, even in wintertime when the snow lay on the high ground. By the time she had cooked an evening meal, she was just exhausted.

They were both working hard and earning little and Hugh was still playing in his band so she was often left on her own. Hugh was young and possibly not really ready for the responsibilities of married life. He changed little in his own life style and made arrangements without consulting Pat, often just informing her what he would be doing and leaving her to deal with it. When they went out on Saturdays it was with the band and Sundays and Christmases were usually spent at Hugh's parents' house. Life settled into a tiring round of sameness and fatigue which gradually wore Pat down. She began to long for a life of her own, for independence, for something more exciting than what she was experiencing. She didn't know just then that she would only truly have a life of her own when she gave it up to God, that she had been made, not for independence but for total dependence on Him, or that the only really exciting life was one spent in His service.

So after just four years of married life, Pat left Hugh and left Northern Ireland, encouraged by friends who thought she was just right to head off for pastures new. Hugh was heartbroken and angry and dealt with his turbulent emotions by clearing their house of almost all that reminded him of his young bride. He threw away photographs and letters, including the love letter he had sent to her on her wedding day and kept a solitary tiny photograph in his wallet – a picture of Pat when she was just fourteen.

After two weeks of trying out this new found independence, she ended up in London and went to live with her brother, Harold, who by this time was married to Pearl and had a young family. She had no job and spent a hot exhausting day tramping the streets of London. Time after time she heard the discouraging words, "Sorry, we've no vacancies" but towards the end of the afternoon, someone told her that there might be a position in Haymarket, in Central London. Wearily she set out to find the shop, called Burberrys and was ushered in to a big dusty room, where a Turkish man interviewed her. Even though she was tired and dishevelled and not looking her best, the Turkish man's eyes lit up when he saw her. He interviewed her and then said the words she had been longing to hear,

"When can you start?"

"Now!" Pat quickly replied, laughing with relief.

They arranged for her to start the next day and she soon discovered that this was considered to be 'the' place to shop in London. She met film stars and pop stars – saw Mick Jagger and Tommy Cooper – and got on well with her colleagues.

On the outside, life was good and Pat was making a success of her career and she tried very hard to settle but on the inside, she felt numb – she was miserable but couldn't even cry. She kept thinking of Hugh and what she had given up and knew that deep down there would always be a pull back to Hugh and to life in Northern Ireland. Finally, one Sunday afternoon, the tears she had been holding back for so long began to flow and even though she had no relationship with God, she cried out to Him in her despair,

"Oh God, if You put my life right, I'll give myself to You!"

The prayer had hardly left her lips when Harold knocked at the door and went in. He had obviously seen her sadness and had decided that something had to be done.

"You miss Hugh, don't you?" he asked her.

Pat just nodded her head in assent, too upset to say anything. Harold and Pearl sprang into action and before Pat had time to think too much about what was happening, Pearl had walked with her to a nearby telephone kiosk and stood with her while she phoned Hugh. They arranged to meet the following week in Belfast.

The visit was only possible because Burberrys had given her a few days off to see her family prior to travelling to Germany for the company. They hoped that Pat would work in one of their shops in Germany for an indefinite period and very kindly encouraged her to see her family before taking up this position. God's timing, as usual, was perfect!

For their reunion, Pat decided to wear a wool cream suit with suede accessories. It looked well on her and showed off her healthy tan.

"You're beautiful," were Hugh's first words when they met outside Robbs shop in Belfast centre.

"You're awful! What has happened to you?" was her shocked reply. She couldn't believe how pale and ill Hugh looked. As they talked over a meal she discovered that Hugh had sold their bungalow and moved back into the farm at Ballynure. He had bought himself an expensive sheepskin coat but even that finery couldn't disguise how poorly he looked and he told Pat that he had been ill. They both admitted that they had missed each other and by the end of the evening had arranged that Pat would return, as planned, to London, go on to Germany and they would use the time apart to consider whether or not they should give their marriage another chance.

Pat visited the various members of her family and friends to say her goodbyes and the following Sunday began preparing for her late-night flight back to London. She was getting dressed in her Mother's bathroom when suddenly a Voice spoke to her,

"Don't go!"

She lifted her head in surprise, for there was no one else in the room.

"Don't go!" the Voice came again and this time Pat ran out of the bathroom in fear and panic.

She slipped on the stairs and slid down on her back but even as she did so, she could clearly hear the Voice again,

"Don't go!"

"Dad! Dad! Dad!" Pat cried out in terror as she landed with a thud at the bottom of the stairs.

Her father ran out of the living room and pulled her to her feet.

"What's wrong?" he asked, looking at her terrified face for some clue.

"There's a voice...." Pat could hardly get the words out, "it spoke to me three times, saying, 'Don't go'...."

Joseph wouldn't have called himself a religious man but he feared God and the colour drained from his face. He looked her right in the eyes and with his finger pointing straight at her, he cried,

"Patsy, I'm warning you, don't go!"

That was enough for Pat. As she calmed down and recovered from the fright, she began to realise that she had heard that Voice before but still she didn't recognise the Name of the One who was calling to her. She knew enough, however, to acknowledge that her father was right and she had to obey. She and her Mum went to the telephone kiosk and phoned Harold to tell him that she wasn't going back. She was surprised to find that Harold was greatly relieved – he had felt there was no life in London for Pat and even had a strange sense that some sort of evil was waiting for her but didn't say anything in case she would think he had taken leave of his senses!

Pat wasn't sure what Hugh would think – would he suspect her of being deceptive, of not having any intention of returning, of not having a return flight but of using the threat to make him think he was going to lose her again? She wisely decided to leave that to worry about another time. It was enough to have made her decision to stay. Pat's letter resigning her position at Burberrys was sent off the next day and the door closed on another phase of her life.

## Chapter 11
# Babies

SO ONCE MORE Pat found herself in a city with no work. On Monday night she bought a Belfast Telegraph and scoured its pages for positions. She was delighted to find an opening in a high class furriers called Kartars and accepted the position even though it was only for two days a week. The following night she saw an advertisement for a one-day display position in a shop on the Ormeau Road and she was able to secure that one as well.

Hugh and Pat eventually made contact with each other and agreed to give their marriage another chance. Hugh had sold the bungalow so they had nowhere to live and he had also stopped playing in the band so they had very few friends to help them out. They moved into a flat and put their names on a waiting list for a house and settled down once again to married life.

Not long afterwards, Pat decided that she needed some dental work done, made an appointment and soon found herself lying back in the dental chair, listening to the dentist humming as he did his work. Suddenly she remembered something she had wanted to ask him,

"My teeth bleed now and again – do you think I could have pyorrhoea?"

The dentist had a different possibility for her symptom and enquired,

"Could you be expecting, Mrs Logan?"

"Well, maybe I am," Pat replied, a little tingle of excitement rising up within her.

Once the pregnancy had been confirmed, Hugh had to laugh when Pat remarked,

"Imagine having to go to the dentist to find out that I was going to have a baby!"

Their housing situation was a bit of a worry, as their landlady wanted to renovate the flats and so they had to move out. One of their few friends, June Knowles, stepped into the breach and invited them to move in with her. Fortunately they didn't have to stay too long with June because a one-bedroomed, newly built flat became available in Greenisland. Pat was delighted to discover that the flat opposite was occupied by a young couple, Ethna and Frank Porter, who had just had their first baby shortly before Pat and Hugh moved in.

The weeks passed in a flurry of work, settling into the new flat and preparing for the arrival of the baby, due in the middle of August. The week before the due date, Pat found herself spring-cleaning and tidying, full of energy, a sure sign of the imminent arrival of the Big Day! On the Thursday evening, they had unexpected visitors, an aunt and uncle from Larne and Uncle Billy from Scotland.

"There's nothing in the house for them to eat!" Pat whispered hurriedly to Hugh. "You chat to them and I'll see what I can do."

She rushed around in the kitchen, peeling apples and making pastry and soon an apple tart was in the oven. Then Pat chatted to the guests while Hugh slipped out to the shop for fresh cream. Pat was serving the supper when Hugh's cousin's wife, Eileen, called, wondering if Pat needed any help as it was so close to her due date. Pat brought out another cup and Eileen joined the party. It was little wonder that Pat's labour started later that night.

Pat had already packed a bag for the hospital and Hugh drove her through the empty streets to the Maternity wing of the City Hospital. Apprehension and excitement chased each other around inside as Pat thought about what was about to take place. She was going to be a Mum – how would she cope? What would the birth be like? She had listened to her share of horror stories that young (and not so young) mothers love to tell. All too soon the car drew up at the hospital entrance and Hugh got out to ring the doorbell. A nurse came to the door, took the bag from Hugh and said,

"Say goodbye to your wife, Mr Logan. I'll take it from here."

So began two lonely, pain-filled days. Pat lay all through Friday and into the early hours of Saturday morning, listening to the cries and screams of other women giving birth. Her pains increased in intensity and eventually she was taken to a different room where she was sedated. A lovely senior nurse, who knew what she might have to face, tried to bring her what comfort she could. As the sedation began to take hold, she was asked to sign a consent form, in case they would have to operate. Pat got more and more tired and just wanted it to be all over. When two doctors came to examine her, she was rather confused and asked them,

"Have I had my baby?"

They didn't even reply, just gave her a withering look. Everyone seemed so cold and unhelpful but then the pleasant nurse whom she had met before came back and began to talk to her. The warmth in her voice brought tears to Pat's eyes.

"I'm so pleased to see you!" she whispered.

"Ah, my lamb, is there anything I can do for you?"

"A drink of water, please," Pat begged.

"Oh, darling, I can't" the nurse replied, aware that Pat had to fast in case she needed to go to Theatre.

"Please!" cried Pat, in desperation.

The nurse quickly soaked two cotton buds in water and held them over Pat's lips, letting the water drip into her mouth. She started to laugh as Pat reached out her jaws to suck every last drop, like an alligator snapping at its prey.

Meanwhile Hugh returned home to the flat to await news of the birth. He tried to sit and relax, he tried to do some work but couldn't settle to anything and kept going out to the nearby telephone kiosk to enquire about Pat. Each time a voice would tell him,

"Nothing yet."

Hugh's brother and his wife called to keep him company and they played Monopoly to pass the time, taking breaks to allow Hugh to walk to the phone.

Eventually, late on Friday night, a nurse told him that Pat was going to have a section but gave no other details. Hugh relayed this information to David and June, whose response mirrored Hugh's –

"What's that?" they all wondered, quite worried that there might be something seriously wrong. If the nurse had talked of a Caesarean section, they would have understood better what was happening, but in those days, relatives were not encouraged to ask questions. Pat found out later that the reason for the long delay was because Friday was the 13th and they put off the operation so that the baby wouldn't be born on an unlucky day!

After the operation, Pat was moved into a side ward, still very groggy and not even sure if the baby had been born. Two nurses tucked the bedclothes firmly around her but hardly seemed to notice her. Pat opened her eyes for a brief moment and asked rather fearfully,

"Is my baby alright?"

No one answered and Pat was left with her fears and uncertainty. She drifted off to sleep again and the next thing she knew it was morning and Hugh was bending over her, his face alight with joy and pride.

"Pat, you've given me a son."

Pat looked at him groggily, hardly noticing the beautiful bouquet of flowers he had brought. She gripped his arm and whispered with some urgency in her voice,

"I can't get off the train............ I can't get off the train!"

The colour drained from Hugh's face – he thought there must be something wrong with Pat. Slowly Pat began to realise what had happened and was able to explain to Hugh that she had been wakened up in the middle of a nightmare.

She had been on a journey in a train, surrounded by doctors who were all telling jokes. Pat had to give an answer to one of these jokes or else she was doomed to travel on the train for all eternity. The train was divided into several compartments and each one was filled with doctors, laughing uproariously as Pat walked up the long corridor trying to give them the right answer – but in vain. She was in despair at the thought that she couldn't get off the train!

Gradually the terror faded and she wakened up properly, anxious to see her new son. The nurse brought the tiny baby to her while Hugh was still there and the new parents enjoyed the time spent getting to know this tiny creature who would make such a difference to their lives. They marvelled at how perfect he was, checked that he had ten fingers and toes.

"He looks like you," Pat said.

"But he has your blue eyes," Hugh hastened to add, secretly very pleased that his son looked just like him! They named their new son Richard Hugh but decided to call him Rich for short, as they knew that their lives and their marriage would be greatly enriched by having him.

It would be another five years before Pat would give herself wholeheartedly to God and when that happened, she remembered the strange nightmare she had on the night of Richard's birth. She was able then to make more sense of it and could interpret it from a spiritual point of view. The train, she felt, represented the world and because she had not surrendered her life to God, she was destined to stay on the train, separated from God, for all eternity. She was desperate to get off the train and needed to find the answer. The answer, of course, was Jesus – only in Him would she find peace.

Despite her joy in her newborn son, the next three weeks proved to be difficult weeks. Her wound didn't heal properly – infection set in as a result of being stitched up with contaminated thread and she had to stay in hospital for treatment.

"I just want to get home with my baby," she would cry as she watched other mothers leave with their well-wrapped babies and their proud husbands. She could only hold her little son on the edge of her knees and she just longed to be able to cuddle him in close to her. She knew, of course, that he was getting plenty of love and cuddles from his Dad and his grandparents but it just wasn't the same as being able to wrap him tightly in her own arms.

The three weeks passed and Pat was able to take her little boy home at last. Richard developed into a contented but serious child and sometimes when Pat would try to be playful with him at feeding times, he would sit solemnly in his high chair and just look at his mum as if to say, "Grow up, Mum". It made Pat feel as if he were the grownup and she were the child.

When Richard was eighteen months old, Pat and Hugh discovered that another baby was on the way. The 'troubles' in Northern Ireland were at their height at this time, so they decided it would be wiser to book into a different hospital for the birth. Pat had hoped for an easier confinement than her previous experience but it was not to be. The nursing staff seemed to take some sort of dislike to her and Pat could only put it down to the fact that she was English – the English weren't too popular in some areas of Northern Ireland! After being admitted, she was left alone for what seemed like hours, lying on a most uncomfortable narrow trolley. She was afraid to move in case she fell off. A nurse walked in, totally ignored Pat and walked back out again. She began to wonder if they were going to leave her to give birth on her own!

Some time later, two nursing sisters arrived, accompanied by a doctor who was all gowned up, ready to perform a caesarean. Without saying anything to Pat, the two nurses grabbed her legs and one of them poked her elbow into Pat's side while the other one made rather rude remarks about her feet,

"This one and her big feet!"

Meanwhile their poor patient was trying to cope with contractions as they came, each one fiercer than the one before. The doctor tried to intervene -

"Give her to me," he suggested, "I'll take her to theatre."

But the nurses were determined –

"No, wait, we can handle her," they insisted.

They did agree that he should perform an episiotomy to help matters along.

Pat felt very nervous and intimidated while all of this was going on around her and plucked up enough courage to ask,

"What do you want me to do?"

"Shut your mouth and push!" was the unkind, arrogant response.

A short time later Pat's second son, Robert Jonathan, was born, weighing in at 8lb 2 oz and Pat was brought back to the ward, greatly relieved that her ordeal was over.

The night staff arrived, gave all the mothers a sleeping tablet and whisked the babies away to the nursery. Pat had been taking some sleeping tablets during the pregnancy to help her sleep and so the tablet she was given wasn't as effective as it should have been. In the middle of the night Pat woke up with a start, at first not quite sure just what had wakened her. She soon realised that her sleep had been disturbed by the heart-rending cries of the babies in the nursery.

"The night staff will look after them soon," she consoled herself and rolled over and tried to settle down to sleep again. She lay listening to the high-pitched wails for half an hour but could stand it no longer, got out of bed, put on her dressing gown and made her way slowly to the nursery.

She was horrified by what she found – every baby was crying and not a single nurse was to be seen. Pat searched the cots until she found Jonathan and started to shake with anger when she realised that he was starving and very distressed, moving his head frantically from side to side rooting for food.

Pat marched out of the nursery, down the ward past all the gently snoring mothers to a glass partition that sectioned off the nurses' station. There she found the sister slumped in an armchair, feet up on her desk, also snoring! Pat tapped the window and the nurse nearly fell out of her chair. She was furious when she realised it was a patient who had interrupted her snooze.

"What are you doing out of your bed?" she shouted.

Pat couldn't believe the arrogance of the woman and replied furiously,

"What am I doing out of bed? Who's looking after those hysterical wee babies? They're soaking wet, they're hungry, they're starving! That's why you gave us sleeping pills," she went on, her voice trembling with indignation, "well they didn't work on me!"

The sister had no intention of backing down,

"Get back to your bed," she directed angrily.

"I'm going to attend to my son!" Pat retorted, just as angrily.

"You're not allowed to!" the sister yelled.

"Just try and stop me," was Pat's reply as she turned on her heel and marched back to the nursery, the angry sister hard on her heels.

Once there, Pat found clean nappies and dry vests. She picked up her little sobbing baby, took off his wet clothes, sponged him down, made up a bottle and fed him, shaking with anger that he could have been left in such a state. Her heart bled for the other wee babies whose mothers were sleeping peacefully through their distress. She put Jonathan back into his cot and returned to her bed, still pursued by the nurse but this time trying to make up to Pat and speaking kindly to her.

"Now, come on now, calm yourself. Just get into your bed and have a nice sleep."

Pat did get back into bed but sleep was far from her mind – she lay awake all night, determined that no matter what anyone said, she and her baby were going home in the morning!

When the day staff arrived, they slid the babies out in their cribs, every baby now fast asleep. A baby's bottle was placed on each locker and the nurses called out, "Come along now mothers, wake up and feed your babies!"

One by one they stretched and carefully sat up in bed.

"Oh nurse, I had a lovely sleep," said one mother, as she cuddled her baby and reached for the bottle. A few minutes later, Pat heard her call out,

"Nurse, my baby won't feed, he's too tired!"

Her cry was soon echoed all round the ward as the mothers tried in vain to rouse their sleepy little babies. Jonathan, on the other hand, fed hungrily and Pat was so glad she had tended to him in the night. She was now even more determined to go home and when the doctor visited her on his rounds, she asked if she could go home.

"Do you have anyone at home who could look after you?" he enquired.

"Oh yes," Pat replied, "I have a good mother-in-law."

Hugh arrived at lunchtime with clothes for her and Jonathan and Pat was overjoyed to be able to bring her little son home. Richard had stayed at home with Hugh's mum and came running to see his new brother. Pat presented the new baby to him with a box of chocolates on his tummy for Richard – a suggestion that had been made to her by a lady she had met in the hospital. Richard's face lit up and he leaned over his tiny brother, gave him a kiss on the forehead and whispered,

"What a lovely wee brother, who brought me sweeties."

It was a tender moment, to be treasured up in the heart of the Lord's handmaiden. He would teach her much about love through the gift of these babies - overwhelming, unconditional, heart-rending love.

## Chapter 12
# Wee Girl, You Need Jesus!

THE NEXT TWO years were filled with busy, tiring, happy days. Pat didn't have the money to buy her boys expensive gifts but they made their own fun. On dry sunny days they visited the swing park opposite the shops and wet days were passed happily enough, throwing stones into puddles on the grassy area in front of the house or making a slide by taking the living room door off its hinges and laying it against the back of the settee. How the boys squealed with delight as they climbed to the top of the settee, slid down the smooth door and made a soft landing on the pile of cushions at the bottom. A fall of snow presented even more opportunity for fun – Pat's brother Noel had made a toboggan when he was about eleven years old and had passed it on to Pat, so she would tie the car seat to the toboggan, the two boys would sit on the seat and Pat would pull them along by a rope fixed like a harness around her neck and shoulders.

Despite these happy times, Pat often found herself feeling down. Life sometimes seemed to be an endless round of working, cooking, cleaning, changing nappies, wiping noses and drying tears.

"Is this it?" she began to think, "Life – is this all it's about?"

Sunday was the worst day for household chores and Pat was often left with them while Hugh took the boys to church, more to appease his mother than because of any great desire on his part to attend. Something snapped inside her one Sunday morning as they all set out dressed in their Sunday best.

"You're just a hypocrite," she announced, "the only reason you go to church is because your mother keeps asking if you have been there!"

Hugh didn't reply and simply went on his way, leaving Pat to pull on her rubber gloves and tackle a huge pile of dishes. Her pent up feelings could be held in check no longer and she plunged her hands into the hot soapy water, crying out in desperation to God as she did so,

"God!.... would You show me a church where I could go that isn't interested in fancy hats and clothes...... a place where people gather to worship You!"

She had a strange sense of release as she finished speaking but she had no way of knowing that God was indeed going to answer that heart-felt cry of His handmaiden, though not in a way she would have chosen.

Not long after this Joseph, Pat's father, became ill with suspected cancer and was admitted to Whiteabbey Hospital. May, naturally enough, was distraught at this news, for cancer usually carried a death sentence in those days. Not knowing what to do, she called on a woman who lived nearby. This lady brought her in and listened to her story.

"I think you should ring Sam Workman – he's a local minister," she said.

"But I don't know this man," protested May.

"Listen," the woman urged her, "ten years ago I had cancer. Mr Workman prayed for me and I'm still here today!"

Encouraged by the lady's story, May and Pat walked to the telephone kiosk and rang Mr Workman.

"Well now," he said, "I have to be over in Bangor early this morning and have other calls to make today but I'll do my best to get to the hospital before nine o'clock tomorrow morning."

Reassured by his friendly voice and his promise to visit Joseph, Pat and May made their way home.

The next night, May went to see Joseph. He was still feeling the effects of the sedation but was able to tell her that there had been about a dozen ministers round his bed that morning. May wasn't sure if that was true or simply the effects of the drugs but Joseph went on to say,

"One minister prayed a lovely prayer for me – he prayed 'Please Lord, don't let the doctors find what they are looking for.'"

When the doctors did their rounds later on, Joseph was amazed to hear their report,

"Mr Hyde, we opened you up but couldn't find what we were looking for, so we just took out your appendix in case it would give you problems in later life."

Joseph couldn't believe that the doctors used the very same words as the minister who had prayed with him had used! He found out later on that the minister was Rev Sam Workman. He continued to visit Joseph when he returned home and after a few visits, he led him to the Lord.

Pat was greatly impressed by the miracle of healing in her father's life and began to wonder if Reverend Workman could do anything about the problems she had with her throat. She arranged to visit her parents' home when he would be there and told him about the throat ulcers that made her feel quite ill at times. He gave her some advice that would help the blood flow to her throat, then startled her by saying,

"Wee girl, you need Jesus!"

Pat began to cry and tears and mascara began to run down her face.

"I know," she whispered. Her mother hadn't expected this to happen and was rather embarrassed by Pat's emotional response. She tried to hand Pat a hankie but Pat just knocked it out of her hand – she needed Jesus, not a hankie! For the first time in her life, the possibility of a living, meaningful relationship with Jesus was set before her and she found herself desperate to surrender her whole life to Him and enter into that relationship.

She knelt down at her mother's old armchair, asked God to forgive her for sinning against Him and asked Jesus to come into her heart and save her. She would have found it hard to explain why, but she knew instantly that something significant had happened. There was a peace in her heart that had not been there before and that was unlike anything she had ever known before. Now she understood what the old gentleman in London had meant all those years before. Now she realised that the strange peace she had known fleetingly in the laburnum tree could be her daily experience. Now finally, she had met the One whose Voice she had been hearing at crisis moments in her life.

Hugh arrived soon afterwards to collect her and Pat couldn't wait to tell him her exciting news.

"I'm pleased for you," he said rather guardedly and Pat knew what he was thinking - 'but I'm not getting saved!'

All the way home in the car, Pat marvelled at her new-found joy – her heart felt glowing and warm. She was amazed by what had happened and couldn't believe the peace she felt. She kept thinking over and over, 'I'm born again, how wonderful.' Hugh wasn't so sure about it all,

"We'll see how long you keep it," he said.

"I don't know, Hugh," Pat replied, "something has happened inside of me and it's real."

She noted the date – 19th August 1970 – and would remember it for the rest of her life. She began attending the church where Sam Workman ministered and discovered that God had answered her kitchen sink prayer – it was a church where people gathered to worship the Almighty God and fancy hats and clothes just didn't seem to matter.

## Chapter 13
# Moving On

THE HUGE BONFIRE crackled and whooshed as Pat and Hugh stood watching the celebrations on the eleventh night the following year. Since coming to live in Northern Ireland, Pat had got used to the bonfires and marches and bands that took place in July each year and had brought the two boys to join in the fun. The neighbours all gathered round the fire – it was quite a social occasion – and one of them said to her,

"Did you hear about the new houses being built in Eden in Carrickfergus, with free carpet in the living room?"

Hugh had always insisted that he wouldn't live in Carrickfergus, so Pat was greatly surprised to hear him reply,

"Maybe we should go and look at them."

They made arrangements to go and visit the show house and were very impressed by it, though Pat really felt drawn to the four bungalows that were being built nearby.

"There's no point in looking at those," said Hugh, "we couldn't afford one of the houses, so don't even think of the bungalow."

Normally Hugh's word would have been enough for Pat but there was just something about the idea of those bungalows! She decided to take a look at them and walked over to the first one. It was just grey breezeblocks and wooden floorboards but Pat sensed something as she stood in what would eventually be the living room. That peace she had known before filled her heart and she knew that God had drawn her to that place. She very wisely said nothing to Hugh – just waited to see what God would do.

The following week the two of them were shopping in Belfast and Hugh shocked Pat by suggesting that they should call in with the estate agents. A young man came from an office at the back of the building and asked if he could be of any help.

"We'd like to see the plans for the bungalows being built on the Trailcock Road in Carrickfergus," said Hugh.

"It's right there beside you," he told them, pointing to a plan on the wall, "but I'm afraid you're going to be disappointed because they're all taken."

They examined the plan and Hugh pointed to another group of four bungalows also shown on the plan, separated from the original four by a small road.

"What about these?" asked Hugh.

"Oh they decided not to build them," was the answer.

Just at that moment, Pat felt as though someone had lifted her arm and placed her forefinger on one of the bungalows. She heard herself say,

"That's a pity because that one would be just lovely!"

As the words came out of her mouth, she realised that she wasn't even sure which one she had pointed to! With her heart in her mouth, she took a good look and realised that she was pointing at a bungalow on a corner site on the other side of the road.

She could hardly believe what happened next – the estate agent looked up, adjusted his glasses and said,

"Which one? Oh that one! Hold on a moment. I'll go and check...... just have to make a phone call."

He left Pat and Hugh looking at each other in a bemused sort of way – not entirely sure what was going on. The agent made a call, came back and asked them if they could call back later. Hugh explained that they were on their way home but arranged to ring the agent later on that evening.

They collected the boys from Hugh's mother who had been minding them and as soon as they arrived at their own home, Hugh ran down the road to the telephone kiosk to make the call. He arrived back about ten minutes later, plumped himself into an armchair beside the fire, leaned forward with his chin resting in his hands and exclaimed in amazement,

"We have just bought a bungalow and we have no money to pay for it!"

Despite the fact that Pat's relationship with God was still in its early stages and Hugh didn't even know God, He had it all in hand. When Hugh's mother heard the news, she offered to loan them £200 for the deposit and they accepted gratefully, though they weren't sure how they would manage to pay it back to her.

So the building began and they watched the house take shape with great excitement. As with many building projects, there were problems with the builders. Their difficulties were exacerbated by the fact that Pat became pregnant again during this period but unfortunately lost the baby, probably because of the stress of the situation.

Satan really seemed to have it in for this young couple.

At last the longed for moving day arrived. Pat was so excited about moving into her new home. They had made arrangements for the furniture to be brought at the Easter weekend when Hugh would be off work and others would be free to help them.

Pat wanted everything to be spick and span so she had gone up to the house earlier. She was standing cleaning the front room window when she noticed some strange goings-on in the road outside. The son of the farmer, whose land bordered the development, was setting trestles down in the middle of the drive and then putting a large plank across the trestles!

"Whatever is he doing?" Pat wondered as she watched him, "That blocks the way into our drive."

They discovered later that the farmer had been in dispute with the builders about the driveway and he had chosen the most inconvenient moment to make his protest.

There was little they could do about it – just resigned themselves to having to carry their furniture further than they had intended. To make matters worse, the promised help couldn't come and Pat and Hugh had to lift all the heavy wardrobes and other items down a long flight of stairs in the Greenisland house and then from where they managed to park the van to their new bungalow.

Pat really shouldn't have been doing heavy lifting like that because less than a week earlier, she had suffered an early miscarriage. She had little time to grieve for the loss of this tiny baby. Moving house and looking after two young children made her life just too busy – she had to get up and keep going. She really hoped that life would return to normality after they had settled in but it was not to be. By the summer time she realised (without having to visit the dentist!) that she was expecting again and the farmer chose that time to make his feelings about the driveway obvious once again. As Pat was fighting the nausea of the early weeks of pregnancy, the sickness was made much worse by an awful smell. The farmer kept pigs and was allowing the foul-smelling pig manure to flow into a stream which ran from the hills, past the bungalow on the other side of the stream. Pregnancy had heightened Pat's sensitivity to smell and she spent most of the summer lying on the settee in the living room.

That summer the Lord's handmaiden learnt that belonging to the Lord didn't guarantee an easy life – far from it. She became increasingly aware of the existence of the enemy – the one who constantly wages war in whatever way he can against those who serve the King. He fought a huge battle that summer to bring Pat down and make her miserable, targeting Hugh and the children as well.

Both Hugh and Jonathan broke limbs that summer. Hugh had taken the boys up Ballygally Head and was carrying the weary little boy down again. As they came down a particularly steep part, Hugh slipped and they both rolled over. Hugh fell on top of Jonathan and his arm was broken. He was still in plaster when Hugh broke his leg playing a lunchtime game of football.

"What is going on?" Pat often wondered, as one thing after another seemed to go wrong.

Despite all the problems, Pat's belief that she was in the place where God wanted her to be was reinforced when a neighbour visited her. Margaret lived in the bungalow on the opposite corner and when she realised that Pat wasn't feeling well, she began to visit regularly. When they got to know one another a little better, she asked Pat,

"How did you manage to procure this bungalow?"

"We just bought it," was Pat's reply.

"You know," Margaret informed her, "my husband and I tried to buy this bungalow, a minister and a policeman also tried to buy it. We were told that it wasn't going to be built so we bought elsewhere."

Pat could give Margaret no answers to the mystery but deep down in her heart she sent a prayer of thanks to her heavenly Father for confirming that they had done the right thing. She didn't understand at the time but God was not just moving them on physically, He was also moving them on spiritually. That little bungalow would see much blessing but first its occupants' hearts had to be prepared and their wills made obedient to His.

Chapter 14
# A New Lawn and a Stalled Car

PAT LAY ON the settee, fighting nausea as usual. She was fed up – it seemed as though she had been looking at the bare, freshly painted walls of the living room forever. She wanted desperately to go out but felt too sick to get up. Above all she was lonely, as she hadn't made any close friends. So she cried out to God,

"Dear God, somehow get me out to church!"

The next day was a bright sunny Sunday and Hugh took the boys to church as usual. Pat relaxed in a warm bath, put on a new dressing gown in an attempt to cheer herself up and, once Hugh had returned, struggled into the kitchen to make lunch.

Suddenly they heard a knock at the front door. Hugh opened it to find a friend from work called Pauline and her friend, Eileen. They were dressed for summer in flowing dresses and picture hats and to Pat it seemed as though their faces shone. Hugh greeted them and then Pauline said,

"We've just returned from church and realised that your wife wasn't there. We thought we would call and see how she was. We wondered if she would like to come with us to the evening service?"

Pat was both amazed and delighted that God had answered her prayer so quickly. The two girls became good friends, taking Pat to church every Sunday evening and to the Bible Study every Tuesday evening. They even provided the name for the baby she was expecting. One evening, she was helped out of the car by a tall, fair-haired young man.

"Let me introduce you to James," said Pauline.

Pat heard nothing more of the conversation – she was saying the name 'James' over and over in her head.

"That's what we'll call our baby if it's a boy!" she thought excitedly.

She could hardly wait to get home to tell Hugh and she was delighted when he agreed with her.

"Oh Pat," he said, "that would be wonderful. He'd be named after my father."

Hugh's father had died in 1966.

Pat had learnt by this time that it was a good idea to check things with God, so later that night she did just that and the answer she received was,

"Name him James Matthew Logan."

Pat felt sure that God had something special for this baby, though of course she wasn't entirely certain that she would have a boy. That was confirmed for her on 15th March 1972 when she delivered a brown-eyed, dark haired, beautiful son who weighed in at 7lb 13 oz. Her experience in hospital was much better this time than with the other two babies and it wasn't long before James was home in the bungalow at Trailcock Road, completing their little family.

Pat was anxious that her boys would share her faith and often talked to them about the Lord as she put them to bed. One particular evening she referred to Jesus' statement that faith as small as a mustard seed could move mountains.

"If we have faith and believe God with all our heart," she declared, "then we could say to a mountain, 'Be removed' and it would be removed."

Richard, who was about six at the time, lay in his bed and thought about what his mum had just said.

"You mean even the Knockagh could be removed if we ask God to remove it?" he enquired, sounding quite excited at the idea.

Pat assured him that what she had said was true, though she had never heard of any actual mountain which had been removed in that way! At that time the Knockagh mountain could be seen from the boys' bedroom window and was clearly visible on that sunny spring evening. Richard asked the question again and Pat gave the same answer so he and Jonathan climbed up on to the bed to look out at the mountain. Suddenly Richard squealed,

"Mum! It's gone! The Knockagh's gone!"

Pat got up from the low stool where she had been sitting and made her way over to the window to see what he meant. Sure enough, the Knockagh mountain had been removed! While she had been talking to the boys, an evening mist had rolled in and completely blotted out the mountain. The boys rolled on the bed in fits of laughter and though Pat joined in, a more serious sense of awe filled her heart as she thought of the miracle her God had done to help grow faith in the hearts of two little boys in a bedroom in Carrickfergus.

"If only a similar faith could grow in Hugh's heart," she thought.

Later that evening Hugh went into the bedroom to say goodnight to the boys. He tucked them in and gave them their usual goodnight kiss. As he did so, little Jonathan looked up at him and said,

"Dad, why aren't you saved?"

Hugh made no reply but in her heart Pat prayed that God might use the words of even a four year old to bring Hugh to Himself.

In the months that followed, Pat decided to ask every Christian she met to pray for her husband's salvation but it seemed that the more prayer went up, the harder things became in the home. The enemy was hard at work! Then one day in May, while she was praying, she heard the Voice again, giving her a clear instruction,

"Go and speak to Mr Workman after church on Sunday night and ask him to come and speak to Hugh about his soul."

Pat did so and was a little frustrated when Mr and Mrs Workman told her,

"You're too anxious, wee girl, go home and pray for him."

She continued praying and got the same instruction to go to Rev Workman and got the same reply from him. This happened on three separate occasions so when God told her to ring the minister first thing on Monday morning, she didn't understand what God was doing.

"Look, God," she prayed, "I've done what You've told me three times and all they say is to go home and pray. Now You tell me to ring him first thing on Monday morning to come and visit Hugh."

"Now, Lord, if this is of You and not the enemy sending me on a wild goose chase, You make me land on my feet tomorrow morning on the floor from the bed, without me having to sit up and throw my legs out over the side of the bed. I mean it Lord," she added, "otherwise I'm not ringing Mr Workman!"

With that she committed herself to God as she usually did, got into bed and very quickly fell asleep. The next thing she knew, she was wakening up from a deep sleep, swaying to and fro, after landing on her two feet at the side of the bed! As she rubbed the sleep from her eyes, she began to laugh and laugh. There could be no mistake – God had responded to her prayer and her faith.

She made breakfast for the family and bathed baby James while Hugh left the other two boys to school. As she looked in the hotpress for fresh clothes for James, God's Voice spoke again with renewed urgency,

"Hurry up, you'll miss Mr Workman!"

"I'm hurrying, Lord, I'm hurrying," Pat replied.

She strapped James into his pram, ran down the Trailcock Road and hurried across the busy main road to the telephone kiosk.

When she asked to speak to Rev Workman, his wife replied,

"Oh, my dear, you have just missed him."

It was just all too much for Pat and she began to cry down the phone, pouring out her tale of woe – her concern for Hugh's salvation, her earnest prayers, the clear instructions from God, her disappointment at being told just to pray.

"Pat, my dear," said Mrs Workman sympathetically, "we didn't know you were going through all this!"

She paused for a moment and then spoke quickly,

"Hold on........I think Sammy must still be in the garage..... I can hear the car."

With that she dropped the phone and ran to fetch her husband. When he came to the phone and told Pat that his car had stalled or he would already have gone, she recognised God's hand in it all. Sometimes even stalled cars can be part of His plan! Reverend Workman was free to visit Hugh on Tuesday afternoon and hope and faith sprang up in Pat's heart when she realised that Hugh had booked that day off work to lay a new lawn. She would never have thought that a new lawn and a stalled car would play important roles in bringing Hugh to Christ!

Pat found it hard to concentrate on her window dressing job that Tuesday morning.

She hadn't told Hugh that the minister was coming and wondered how he would react when he found out. Hugh picked her up at one o'clock and had the dinner all prepared, keeping warm in the oven drawer. Pat still didn't say anything and began to worry a little that Mr Workman might mention her frantic phone call. She wasn't sure either how she should react when he came in – should she look surprised to see him?

Just as she went to lift the dinner out, Mr Workman arrived and started up a conversation with Hugh in the garden. Pat went ahead and fed the boys. In a little while, much to Pat's embarrassment, Hugh popped his head round the kitchen door and said,

"Here's your mate to see you."

"What a way to speak about a minister," thought Pat as Rev Workman put his head round the kitchen door too. Pat needn't have worried about what the minister might say – he just started chatting in a friendly natural way and Pat was able to respond in the same way and invite him inside.

The two men went through to the living room, leaving Pat shaking with nerves in the kitchen. She was hungry but felt too sick to eat and she thought it best not to offer Hugh his dinner just yet so she slipped into the living room and sat down quietly at the other end of the room. She had done all she could – now she could only wait and pray silently.

She was amazed at how easily God led the minister to open up the conversation to spiritual things.

"Do you do any preaching yourself, Hugh?" he asked.

"Me? I'm not even saved," came the honest reply.

That was all it took and an hour later, the two men were still talking. Realising that by this time Hugh must be starving, Pat very tentatively offered Rev Workman a cup of tea.

"I thought you'd never ask!" he replied.

Even cups of tea couldn't disturb the intense conversation and soon Pat heard Mr Workman ask,

"Will you take Him, Hugh?"

Pat glanced at Hugh, sitting on the edge of his seat, hands clasped and face white and held her breath as she waited for Hugh's quiet reply,

"I will."

Pat had often wondered how she would react when Hugh gave his life to the Lord – would she shriek with delight....... jump up and down............ cry? In the event, she just sat there, unable to move while a great wave of relief and thanksgiving swept over her. She brought out the well-warmed dinner and another cup of tea for Rev Workman. She hardly noticed that the meal was dried out – so great was the joy in her heart that it tasted like manna from heaven. Now the handmaiden had a partner whose life purpose matched her own – to serve the King of Kings and Lord of Lords. Things would never be the same again in the little bungalow in Carrickfergus.

## Chapter 15
# Provider and Revealer

FROM EARLY ON in her relationship with God, Pat determined to get to know Him intimately and so she decided to clear out the cloakroom to use it as a closet for prayer. About the same time they decided to change the bedrooms around as the boys and all their toys no longer fitted into the smaller bedroom. She knew that their rosewood and mahogany bedroom suite would fit into the new bedroom but Pat was upset when she saw how threadbare the carpet was.

"Lord, what are we going to do?" she enquired. "We have no money to buy a new carpet."

She thought no more of it, just continued to get things ready for the move. She looked affectionately at the shocking pink covers on their bed and congratulated herself once more on how well they looked with the rich, dark furniture.

Around this time, Hugh happened to be chatting to his friend in work, a lovely Christian man called John White who had befriended them and mentioned Pat's plans for the cloakroom. A few days later, John arrived into work with a piece of carpet.

"I thought it might do for the cloakroom where Pat prays," he said.

Hugh thanked him for his kindness and brought the carpet home to Pat, who immediately realised it was the answer to her prayer.

"Never mind the cloakroom," she told Hugh excitedly, "it will fit the boys' bedroom for us to move into. It's in much better condition than the old carpet."

So that night they made a start, laid the carpet and shifted the furniture. Pat brought through her bedcovers and suddenly realised that shocking pink covers were going to clash terribly with a brown and orange carpet! It just looked awful and she told the Lord so!

The following day Hugh phoned her from work and at the end of the call said, "Oh, by the way, John gave me a brown paper parcel for you."

"I know what it is!" Pat replied. "It's an orange bedcover."

"How could you possibly know that?" Hugh asked in bewilderment.

"Tear a corner of the parcel and see," Pat commanded.

Hugh did as she asked and in some amazement said down the phone, "It's orange!"

Hugh resisted the temptation to open the parcel until he went home and when they looked together, there was a replica of Pat's shocking pink bedcover, only in orange! She wasted no time in changing the covers and felt that God, her Great Provider, was laughing along with her as she did so.

Pat and Hugh settled into their new home and the new school term began. They were very happy when some neighbours agreed to an arrangement to collect each other's children from school on alternate days. They taught Richard never to leave the school gates until he was collected and for a while everything worked very well.

Since Hugh had trusted the Lord, he had begun to share his faith. He heard in work about a woman who was dying in a backslidden state and God gave him a burden for her. He and Pat told Sam Workman about her and when he visited her in her home at Greenisland, the minister had the great joy of leading her back to the Lord.

The lady died soon afterwards and Hugh made plans to go to the funeral.

"I'm glad Pat doesn't have to collect Richard from school," he thought as he drove along, "it's not her turn."

Unfortunately the neighbour had forgotten about his responsibility and poor little Richard was left standing alone at the school gates. He waited and waited, hoping that someone would come but eventually he realised that everyone else had gone home and he wasn't sure what to do. All the warnings about waiting at the gates were forgotten – he just wanted to get home! So he set off up the road, looking at every car that passed in case it was his lift.

Suddenly he saw his Dad's car on the other side of the main road. He dashed out into the road, frantic that perhaps his dad hadn't seen him. There was a great screeching of brakes as an oncoming car tried to avoid hitting him. Hugh hadn't seen Richard run into the road but realised that something had happened and stopped to investigate. He was horrified to discover that Richard had narrowly missed being run over. He returned home with the shaken little boy and then went on to the funeral. Pat clasped Richard close to her, shocked by what had happened and also by what might have resulted had the driver not been able to stop.

Had this incident taken place later on in her Christian life, she would have recognised it as an attack by the enemy, for that morning she had spent a very special time in the Presence of the Lord. Pat had bathed baby James, tidied the house and put him down for a nap. She then sat down to read and pray. She was amazed to discover as she read one of Paul's letters that God's Word became so real to her that she couldn't stop reading. In some mysterious way, she felt part of the scriptures.

"It's as though I'm actually living in them," she thought, as her spirit within responded to the words she was reading.

She read and read until she had completed twelve chapters! She had never before experienced this intimate connection with the Word of God, though something told her that this was the way the Word should be read. In later years she would understand it to be the Holy Spirit descending on His Word.

Pat waited until Hugh returned from the funeral, they had eaten their evening meal and the older boys were tucked up in bed before she tried to explain to Hugh her experience of the morning. As she gave James his bedtime bottle, she told Hugh what had happened to her as she had read the Bible.

"Why don't you read those chapters while I'm feeding James?" she suggested.

Hugh took down his Bible and turned over the pages of the New Testament but, try as he might, he couldn't get any further than John chapter 16.

"Well then, read that instead," Pat advised.

So Hugh read the words spoken by Jesus to His disciples just before His death. As his quiet voice filled the room, Pat lifted her heart in a silent prayer to God,

"Lord, Hugh sounds so humble – it's beautiful to hear. I'd like to know what it would be like to be humble."

Hugh closed the Bible and his thoughts turned to the very disturbing incident earlier in the day..

"You'll have to go down and see those neighbours," he announced, sounding very annoyed, "and let them know what happened. Tell them that our arrangement is off."

"Well, you're the father – you go," Pat retorted.

They tossed this back and forth for a minute or two and then Pat began to feel uneasy. Of course they had every right to be annoyed but their anger didn't sit comfortably with Pat's incredible experience of the morning or with the lovely words they had just listened to.

"Why are we carrying on like this?" Pat said eventually. "We're saved now. God fights our battles. Let's pray about it instead."

Hugh was a comparatively new Christian and still wasn't comfortable with praying aloud, so he instructed Pat,

"You pray."

"Dear Lord," she began, "You are our Heavenly Father so we don't need to go sorting things out with our neighbours –it could just turn into a row. Oh Father – You fight for us."

Suddenly Pat had a strong sense that Someone else was in the room, beside the fireplace.

"Lord, You're in this room," she said in wonder.

As she uttered these words, it seemed that God came even closer and spoke into her heart,

"Lay the baby at the back of the settee."

Very carefully, Pat laid little James at the back of the settee – he didn't even stir. She turned round again, conscious that the Almighty God was there, right in her living room! Suddenly she was overwhelmed by a deep, intense feeling of humility. She fell to her knees – she could do nothing else – and began to weep as the reality of His Presence filled her whole being. Like Mary of old, she began to search for His feet to kiss them. She moved towards Hugh's feet but they were not the feet she was looking for. It was Jesus' feet she wanted to kiss. At this realisation, her weeping intensified.

Hugh had not seen what Pat had seen and didn't know what was going on in her heart to cause such distress. He reached out a hand to comfort her,

"What's wrong, love?" he asked.

"I'm looking for Jesus' feet," was the unexpected reply!

Just at that moment, the Voice came again,

"Look up and sit back on to the settee."

Pat obeyed and in the moments that followed had the incredible privilege of being granted a vision of Jesus Himself. In some mysterious way, although her eyes were closed in prayer, she saw the Lord with utmost clarity. As she watched, the splendour of His image lit up the entire fireplace wall. She found it hard afterwards to describe His beauty – He was smiling, a wonderful, generous smile and it seemed to her that His smiling mouth represented the nations of the earth, the whole wide world. His golden hair gleamed in the Holy Light which also lit up His white robe. That same intense light blinded Pat so that she couldn't see His eyes but she was aware that His arms were outstretched towards her.

As Pat gazed at His majesty, she realised that not even the most famous of all earth's painters or sculptors had ever come close to depicting His glory. What amazed her most of all was the joy she saw on His face – an abundant joy, a fullness of joy, a joy unspeakable and full of glory, a joy she had never seen on any human face and knew she never would. She sat there, transfixed by the joy and the light, her heart bursting with awe and wonder, afraid to move, afraid almost to breathe in case she missed a single second of the glory. She wasn't even aware that Hugh had slipped off to bed – he had no idea of what had happened. The Glory of God remained in the room for about an hour after the vision faded – Pat didn't fully know it but she had been on holy ground, a partaker of an amazing blessing.

As if in a dream, she silently lifted the still sleeping baby, placed him into his carrycot and slid the cot on its stand down to the bedroom. Pat asked God to give her a hymn to describe that experience and she came across the following verse as she searched the Songs of Victory book:

"I have seen a light from Heaven
Past the brightness of the sun,
I have seen the face of Jesus
Tell me not of aught beside
I have heard the voice of Jesus
All my soul is satisfied."

As she thanked God for the hymn, she wondered if perhaps the writer had shared a similar experience to her own – she could certainly identify with his words!

Later that year, one winter morning, they woke to find a blanket of snow lying thick on the ground.

"It's snowing! Let's get our sleighs out!" the boys shouted excitedly.

Hugh and Pat decided to take them to Knockagh Mountain so they all piled into the car, well wrapped up against the winter cold. The sun shone brightly on the glistening snow, almost blinding them as they drove along and Pat was reminded of the intense light of her vision.

"That still isn't as bright as the holy light that shone that night in my living room," thought Pat.

Other people had obviously had the same idea, mostly professional people with their children on sleighs. As Pat listened to the conversation of those around her, she realised that two men, who were skiing, were ballet dancers. They were speaking rather loudly about the previous evening and one of them began to boast,

"Last night I performed before the Queen and had an audience with her!"

Ordinarily a statement like that would have impressed Pat – imagine dancing in front of the Queen and actually talking to her – but no longer. She would have liked to tell that proud dancer,

"Young man, one night in my living room, I had an audience with the King of Kings!"

In Pat's mind, no experience on earth could ever compare with her vision of the Lord of Glory. She had been familiar with His Voice – now she knew something of His Glory.

## Chapter 16
# Handmaiden at Work

"WHAT A LOVELY day," thought Pat, "It's too good to sit inside – I think I'll just take James out into the garden when he wakes up from his nap."

As she sat enjoying the sunshine, a young lad walked past and she noticed a 'Jesus Saves' badge in his lapel. When Hugh returned home from work, she told him what she had seen.

"Why didn't you introduce yourself?" Hugh asked.

"I didn't like to," was Pat's reply.

Encouraged by Hugh's suggestion, Pat looked out for the young man and spoke to him next time he passed. She discovered that his name was Robin Campbell and that he was a new Christian. She went on to explain that they attended Abbott's Cross Church but met in their own home with some friends after church each Sunday evening. They sang together and Sidney Johnston, one of the neighbours, usually preached.

"Could I come to that?" Robin asked.

"You certainly could – you'd be very welcome," was Pat's delighted reply.

A couple of days later, a blind neighbour, John Neill, passed the garden. He told Pat that he and his family had just recently moved into the house behind hers.

"I often hear singing coming from your house," he remarked.

"Yes, that's right," Pat told him, "we have recently got saved."

"Would you mind if I came to your meetings?" he enquired, "I'm a backslider."

Not long after he started attending the meetings, John came back to the Lord and became concerned for his wife's spiritual state. Eventually he asked Pat if she would go and speak to Audrey as he felt that God had begun to deal with her. Pat began to pray for Audrey and the next day, while in her bathroom, God gave her a great burden for Audrey. She cried out to God for her and then set out for the Neills' house. She had never done this sort of thing before and knocked the door in fear and trembling. There was no reply so she returned to the bathroom to pray some more.

Once again she set out for Audrey' home, once again she stood in front of the door in fear and trembling and once again there was no reply! The Lord's handmaiden was not to be deterred, however, so she returned to the bathroom for the third time to pray. Then, claiming the verse in Luke chapter 11, "Knock and it shall be opened unto you", she arrived once more at Audrey's door, determination in every step.

This time when she knocked the door, the door was opened instantly, before she had time to take her hand off the knocker. Pat nearly fell over the threshold. Audrey was a very friendly, sociable person and she was delighted to see Pat.

"Come in, come in," she urged.

Pat was so worked up by this time, that everything just came tumbling out.

"Audrey," she spluttered, "I've been seeking God about your soul. Do you want to get saved?"

"Oh yes, I do," she answered and Pat could hear the longing in her voice. It wasn't long before the two women were kneeling before God as Pat led Audrey in the sinner's prayer, repenting of her sin, seeking God's forgiveness and calling on God to save her – and He did. With tears in their eyes, the two women embraced, not just friends now but sisters in Him. In Heaven, the angels threw a party, rejoicing at the new birth of another soul – did they also rejoice that the King had found a handmaiden who would do His bidding and not be easily turned aside from her assignments?

Audrey, in her turn, spoke to another neighbour, Anne Comins, about her faith. She invited her to a Gospel Mission and she agreed to go. On the night in question, Audrey couldn't go so Anne went with Pat and Hugh. When the appeal was made, she went out to the front and trusted in the Lord. Shortly after this, Audrey's family and Anne's husband and family all became Christians too. More rejoicing in Heaven!

Later that summer, Pat was steeping her nappies in Napisan when Robin Campbell popped his head round the kitchen door. Pat watched as he threw himself down on to the lawn and thought that he looked a bit downcast.

"Ah, Robin, what's wrong?" she asked.

"I'd just love to get a whole lot of children together and have a meeting," he replied, obviously unable to see any way for his vision to be realised.

"Well," Pat called out, "why don't you do just that and bring them back to our lawn. When I get cleared up, I'll help you."

"Oh, really?" he shouted as he jumped to his feet, beaming from ear to ear. He set off like a man on a mission – and what a mission it turned out to be! He returned later in the day with a list of forty or fifty names of boys and girls from the surrounding houses who had agreed to come. He had also got permission from their parents for them to attend the meeting, which he had arranged for the following day from three to four o'clock.

Pat realised that her idea of a few children sitting on her lawn had been a bit small and burst out laughing.

"Boy, Robin," she announced, "you and I need to pray and seek God. This is serious and we need God's guidance. It's unlikely that these afternoons will all be dry."

The next half hour was spent in prayer, after which they felt led to hold the meetings in Pat's garage so they set to work. Out came the brush and dustpan and they found bricks to hold planks around the garage walls for seats. Robin rushed home and brought back carpet squares to cover the planks and soon it was all ready for the influx the next day. They stood for a moment, admiring their work and then committed it all to the Lord.

The following day at three o'clock, children began arriving from everywhere. They managed to cram them all into the garage and the "Happy Hour" began. Pat started each meeting off with an action-packed chorus that soon became a favourite

– "We may never march with the infantry....." The children stood in the garage and sang their hearts out. Robin would speak to them and when Hugh returned home from work, he would tell them a story about Jesus.

Each meeting ended with a call and response learnt from Arthur Blessit, an American Christian hippie, who had visited their church when he came to Ireland. Arthur was famous for the calling he felt to walk the world, carrying a huge wooden cross. As he walked many asked him,

"What are you doing?"

He was always delighted to explain – telling everyone who asked about Jesus and how He had died on a wooden cross for them. He led many to the Lord as a result. In the meetings he took, he used to call out at the top of his voice,

"Give me a J!"

"J," everyone would shout back.

He would then continue spelling out the letters J E S U S and at the end everyone would shout, "Jesus!"

Pat and Robin decided to include this in the children's meetings and the boys and girls joined in with great gusto.

As Hugh didn't always make it home in time to tell the story, they asked a neighbour, Jean Kennedy to help with the story telling. Jean felt that the work should be publicised and invited a reporter and photographer to write it up in the local newspaper. She also shared it with her church, the Church of the Nazarene, who in turn contacted their Head Office in America. The end result was that the Church of the Nazarene felt that they should begin a church in Carrickfergus and proceeded to set this in motion. They used a renovated chicken shed until the church was built. How wonderful to realise that a new church was planted all because a young man felt a burden for the lost souls of the children in his area and an obedient handmaiden was prepared to help him. The meetings ran for that summer and many of the boys and girls gave their lives to the Lord.

Although Pat was only a young Christian, God was teaching her some very valuable lessons. When the Church of the Nazarene decided to continue the children's meetings on a Saturday morning, Jean sent her daughter to Pat's house to ask if she would help with the meetings. Pat's immediate reaction was to say, "Certainly" but something (or was it Someone?) held her back.

"Tell your mum I'll pray about it," she replied instead.

Pat got down on her knees straight away, thinking in her heart,

"Well, why not? Jean helped us out with our meetings in the garage. Now that they're being held in the Church of the Nazarene, maybe I should help them out."

She laid it all out before the Lord and to her surprise the answer was "No."

"No?" she questioned, "but….." She got no further. God could see her heart and knew what she was thinking,

"Jean helped me out – how can I say I won't help her out?"

The Lord's response to her "Why?" surprised her.

"Because you only want to save your face. I want you to obey me and My will for you. My will is for you to stay in the house on Saturday morning."

So Pat wrote a note to Jean explaining why she couldn't help out and just hoped that Jean would understand. On the following Saturday morning, three people arrived at her door, very much in need of help. How thankful she was that she had asked the Lord about the matter and obeyed His will. She was beginning to discover that the enemy had very subtle ways of distracting her from God's path for her life. What had seemed a good thing to do, had turned out to be the wrong thing entirely. It was a lesson that not many learn so early in their journey with Him.

During that summer Pat and Hugh often wondered what plans God had for their lives. There were about fifteen people attending their Sunday evening meeting and they were thoroughly enjoying ministering to the forty or fifty children who crowded in to their garage through the week. Was God leading them into children's work? They had no idea but knew that He would reveal His will in His time – meanwhile they would just go on serving Him.

Chapter 17
# Knowing Him

PAT WAS SITTING on the settee in the living room watching Hugh painting the door when he began to tell her about a man he had met in the church. Jimmie Carson often gave out hymn books at the door and always greeted everyone with a big smile and a warm handshake.

"His face just shines," said Hugh, "he really seems to have something special."

Hugh went on to make a statement that in ordinary circumstances should have upset Pat or at the very least startled her.

"You know, whatever that man has, I want it – even if it means you and me separating to receive it," he announced.

Far from being upset, Pat recognised it as a great spiritual longing in Hugh's heart and found her own heart being stirred too.

"I want it too," she thought.

At that point, they weren't even sure what "It" was but both of them were conscious of there being something more in the Christian life to be sought after and not long afterwards Pat got the opportunity to speak to Jimmie.

"My husband's a great admirer of yours," she said to him as she accepted the hymnbook he held out to her.

"Who's your husband?" he asked.

"Hugh Logan," Pat replied, "he recently got saved."

"Where do you live?" was the next question.

"Carrickfergus."

"I live there too. Do you make a good cup of tea?" he enquired with a big smile.

"An old English one," Pat laughed.

"I'll maybe call and see you both some evening," he said as Pat moved on into the church.

Much to Pat and Hugh's disappointment, there was no visit from Jimmie that week and so when Pauline brought her to church the following week, Pat reminded Jimmie of his promise.

"You were to call and visit with us," she said as Jimmie greeted her at the door.

"Ah yes – where is it you live?" he asked and Pat gave him their address.

"Right, will you be in on Saturday night?"

"Yes," Pat replied.

"Good. Have you any children?"

"Three boys."

"Well, keep them up and I'll be round."

The following Saturday, everyone in the Logan household was excited. Hugh bathed the boys and put them into their pyjamas, while Pat got the supper ready. Soon Jimmie knocked at the door and was ushered into the living room. He had brought his daughter, Muriel, to play the guitar and a girl called Liz to sing. Jimmie played the accordion and they all started to sing. Pat plucked up enough courage to ask if she could tape the evening as she wanted to learn the new choruses that were being sung in the church at that time. They spent a wonderful two hours praising God after which they enjoyed Pat's supper. Jimmie prayed for the boys and they went off to bed, then Jimmie opened up the Word of God. Pat and Hugh sat enthralled as they listened to this man of God share what he had learnt of the Scriptures. It was the first of many such nights when they and others would meet to worship God and learn more of Him.

It was from Jimmie that they learnt about the work of the Holy Spirit in the Christian's life and the need to be sanctified wholly before God. They soon realised that this explained the "It" they had seen in Jimmie's life which they were desperate to know for themselves. When they listened to him preach, they knew that the Spirit of God who indwelt him also enlightened his mind and gave him fresh insight and understanding of the Word and they sensed that the same Spirit who indwelt them caused a response to rise in their own hearts, so that they heard the Word with joy and with renewed determination to obey it.

Pat also learnt the importance of waiting on God and obeying Him in one of these meetings. On that occasion, Jimmie had brought a well-known Scottish preacher, Raymond McKeown, to pray with them. He led them in a wonderful worship time before the boys went to bed and then they settled down to pray. The room was warm so Hugh had taken off his cardigan and put it over the back of the chair. As they waited Pat sensed God say to her, "Cover your head." The room was so quiet that she didn't want to disturb the silence by going out to find something, so she just crept over to where the cardigan was and put it on her head! Their waiting and Pat's obedience were richly rewarded when the Presence of God descended on the room. Pat was reminded of the words of a hymn:

"From the world of sin and noise
And hurry I withdraw,
For the small and inward voice
I wait in humble awe.
Silent am I now and still,
Dare not in Thy Presence move,
To my waiting soul reveal
The secret of Thy love."

So each visit found them opening themselves more and more to God's Word and becoming more and more sensitive to the Holy Spirit. They began to recognise His Presence and He made their God very real to them. They had never known anything like this before – God Himself was mighty in their midst. They didn't want the meetings to end – they could have gone on praising God all night. These were wonderful days for the handmaiden – days when she experienced something of the intimacy that was possible with the King, days when He touched her life with His fire, filled her with His Spirit and empowered her for the work He had planned for her.

It was in the context of these meetings that the King would introduce His handmaiden to one vital part of her assignment. Jimmie began to talk to the group about Revival – a special time of great blessing when God would do an extraordinary work among a particular people or in a particular place.

"Can I call in tonight?" he asked one day when he called at the house. "I have a tape I want to play to you. It's about the Revival in Lewis in 1948."

As Pat listened to a Faith Mission minister called Duncan Campbell tell the story of what had happened in Lewis, she sensed the Presence of God so strongly that it lasted with her for the rest of the week. Both she and Hugh felt that their souls had been smitten by God. Duncan Campbell told how the power of God had descended on believers and non-believers alike. She heard how many of the Christians had been moved to pray, pleading with God for His blessing in barns, fields, behind hedges and in churches. Her heart was touched as she listened to the story of two old women who spent nights in prayer, sacrificing sleep to plead with God to fulfil His promises. She was thrilled to realise that in answer to these prayers, God came.

The entire island was gripped by the Spirit of God. To some He came as the Comforter, bringing joy and peace to their hearts but to others He came as the One who convicts of sin and speaks of judgement. Many repented and found Jesus as their Saviour. Some spent days flat on their faces, prostrate before a Holy God, crying out for mercy before they found the peace they so longed for. What an amazing story it was!

Something in Pat's spirit resonated with what she heard and a great longing rose up within her – could God come to Northern Ireland as He had to the island of Lewis? Could God come to Carrickfergus in power? Could God come to Trailcock Road and pour out His blessing in the same way? She knew the answer to her questions – "Yes of course He could!" Somewhere deep in her heart there arose the beginning of what would become a lifelong cry, "Come, Spirit of God, come in power." The King had handed out the assignment – one of His handmaiden's most important tasks would be to pray for Revival.

## Chapter 18
# An Obedient Heart

SOON AFTERWARDS PAT had a little foretaste of what Revival could be like. She went to the church Bible Study one week with John and Audrey Neill and Jim and Anne Comins. Much to her delight, the visiting preacher spoke on Revival and Pat's heart was stirred within her. As the closing hymn was being announced, Pat sensed the Lord speaking to her,

"I want you to go out to the front and kneel down in front of the pulpit."

She began to shake – she recognised that Voice! It was the same Voice that had spoken so forcefully to her in her mother's bathroom, telling her three times not to go to London. Her heart pounded and she wished Hugh had gone with her. She hadn't seen Jimmie Carson in the meeting either so there was no one with whom she could check this out.

As all these thoughts ran through her mind, she noticed Audrey shifting in her seat as if she was about to get up.

"If you don't go, I'll ask Audrey!" the Voice warned her.

Suddenly Pat heard herself replying,

"No, You won't. I'll go but only if the first line of this hymn we're about to sing makes me cry. I want to be sure that this is of You and not the enemy sending me out."

The organist began the introduction and Pat ran her eye over the first line - nothing there to make her cry, she thought with some relief. She was totally unprepared for what happened next. She stood up and opened her mouth to join the rest of the congregation when the floodgates just burst – not just tears but torrents of tears! She threw the hymnbook out of her hand and, not caring what anyone thought, ran all the way down the aisle, falling to her knees in front of the pulpit, conscious of nothing but the Holy Spirit hovering over her.

The next thing she heard was the scraping sound of chairs being pushed back as men and women fell to their knees, humbling themselves before God and crying out to Him. Pat could hear heartfelt groans behind her. Two ladies who had not been speaking to each other ended up on their knees.

"Oh Lord, I ask my sister to forgive me for not speaking to her!" prayed one as the other cried out,

"Lord, I'm not worthy to untie her shoe latchet."

They remained there, repenting of their wrong attitudes. Pat realised that the Spirit of God was at work and she was so afraid that someone would quench what He was doing. She sensed in her spirit that the minister had recovered from his shock at what had happened and was about to take control of the situation, possibly by sending those on their knees at the front out to another area.

Suddenly one of the deacons stood up and in a very definite voice said,

"Brother, I believe I have a message from God. You are not......I repeat, you are not to remove these people."

The minister waited for a few moments, as though he was weighing up what had been said and trying to decide what to do. Then he spoke,

"Hold on folks," he announced, "you people at the back, keep your seats, while we get those at the front into the counselling rooms."

Pat and the others, some still weeping, were led out and prayed with in another room. Those at the back, behind where Pat had been sitting, remained silent as though rendered speechless. Afterwards she learnt that they had stayed like that for some time. It seemed as though a line had been drawn in the room and those in front of Pat were impacted in a mighty way, while those behind had remained untouched – one of the mysterious ways in which the Spirit of God chooses to work. She often wondered what would have happened if they had all stayed in the same room – would the Revival she had begun to long for and pray for have begun there and rippled out across Northern Ireland? Or had God just given His handmaiden a little taster to inspire her to pray with even greater passion for an outpouring of His Spirit?

She would never know what might have been but she did learn some valuable lessons from that night. One lesson was that when the Holy Spirit moves like that, He always changes lives. Some of them gathered in Pat's house afterwards and Hugh went to fetch Jimmie Carson so that they could share their experiences with him. How thrilled they were to realise the work that God had done among them – many little mini-Revivals had taken place in their own hearts. Jimmie committed them to God in prayer and they all left for home. On his way out, he turned to Pat and Hugh and remarked,

"The Prayer Meeting at church in the morning will be full to the brim!"

His words came true and Pat learnt another lesson – when the Holy Spirit moves, the prayer life of a church, or indeed an individual, is wonderfully deepened. The experience also taught Pat to fear God greatly and to recognise that praying for Revival was a serious work, which required hearts and lives prepared before God for its arrival.

The following day, in her quiet time alone with God, Pat had much to consider and so she talked it all out with Him. She was greatly burdened by what had happened and decided that she needed to spend time in prayer and fasting so that she might know the heart of God on the matter. She fasted each day until six o'clock in the evening and spent many hours of each day in prayer. She waited in silence before Him, giving her all to the Lord, often weeping as she waited for His word.

"What do You want me to do?" she wondered.

"This is too serious," came another thought.

"You are real. The people weren't ready for You," she told the Father and her heart was saddened by that realisation. She sensed that things could never be the same again and she sought for God's direction. In the days that followed, she earnestly asked God to reveal His will but it was not until the end of the week that she knew His heart for her.

"I want you to spend Tuesday evenings from now on in your living room, praying for Revival."

She told Hugh how she felt that God was directing her in this way and he committed to pray for God's direction for him too. After seeking God's face, he was convinced that he should join Pat and give himself to prayer for Revival too. It was a decision that was not taken lightly as they were both acutely aware that their actions might well be misunderstood. It was all too possible that many who attended the meeting might think they had left in some sort of fit of pique but they were determined to obey the Voice of God and to leave the consequences in His hands.

The following Tuesday Pat met Audrey and as they were saying their goodbyes Audrey shouted,

"See you later at the Bible Study!"

"I won't be going," was Pat's reply.

"You're not going? Why not?" Audrey asked, looking at Pat in disbelief. Pat tried to explain but it was obvious that Audrey was finding it hard to understand why Pat would not want to go to the Bible Study. She was afraid that Pat was being deceived and Pat knew that she had no way to convince her – only time would tell if God had really spoken to Pat about this part of His plan for her life.

Hugh and Pat found that this pattern would be repeated many times in their journey with the King – their desire to seek His will and to obey it entirely led them to be misunderstood often and even cost them friendships. Sometimes what God required of them didn't make sense to other people and so the new path God called them to walk wasn't an easy one but they would have chosen no other. As they bowed to His will and humbled themselves before Him, they experienced the joy of the Lord as never before and, in dying to themselves, found victory in Jesus. He was all they had ever hoped for and they were more than willing to let Him lead them. There were tough times of breaking and remaking but the rewards were immeasurable. Their decision was vindicated when many other young people began to gather on a Tuesday evening in their home to join them in their cry for God to break through in power in their town and beyond.

Pat was also to discover that winning souls for Jesus often required obedience on her part too. The circumstances surrounding the conversion of Mrs Sutton were a great example of this principle at work. It had all begun with the previous owner of Mrs Sutton's home, a small Orlit bungalow opposite Pat and Hugh's home. This lady, whom some of the locals called 'Granny' was a wealthy, elderly English woman who had come to Carrickfergus on holiday but stayed on after her husband had become ill and died. As time went by, her behaviour became more and more eccentric. She began to drink and smoke and was usually dressed in a white nightgown on the rare occasions when she ventured outdoors. The children teased her by pretending to be frightened of her and running away when they saw her. She could often be heard shouting at them.

One evening, as Pat was calling the boys in for their evening meal, she noticed that Granny was outside. Pat watched for a moment, interested because this was the first opportunity she had had to see her clearly. She soon realised that something was wrong when she saw her running from her house, looking really afraid and shouting,

"Bomb, the bomb!"

When this happened a second time, Pat decided to go over to speak to her. She felt so sorry for the poor woman.

"Can I be of any help?" she asked.

The lady just waved Pat into the bungalow and gestured towards the cooker. Pat realised that something had blown in the cooker and frightened the other woman.

"Wait there – I'll see if one of my friends can help," Pat instructed her. Pat ran to fetch a neighbour, who was only too glad to fix the cooker.

While he was doing this Pat took a look around. What awful conditions this lady was living in. Despite having enough money for her needs and a home help, the house looked as though it had never been properly cleaned. Large bundles of unopened cigarettes were stacked high all over the room, an overflowing chamber pot (or Jerry) was sitting by the wall, the curtains were closed and the walls were stained with nicotine. Pat's heart went out to her but she never got the opportunity to offer her any help or talk to her because by the next morning, the lady had gone and the bungalow was completely empty. Pat never heard what had happened to her and that day made a vow to God,

"Whoever lives in that bungalow again, I'll tell them of Jesus."

Some time later Mrs Sutton settled into the bungalow. She was another elderly lady, petite and old-fashioned. Pat would often meet her when she was out walking with little James and kept her vow to tell this neighbour about Jesus. She did so on numerous occasions over a period of about two years without any response on Mrs Sutton's part.

But God was setting everything in place – just one final act of obedience was required from His handmaiden. Hugh and Pat had been renting a television set but the Lord began to speak to Hugh, telling him that it had to go. Pat enjoyed the programmes and found it hard when Hugh told her what he believed God was saying to his heart. She watched with something akin to grief as the television was carried out and taken away in a van but she gave her mourning over to God and knew that she would know His blessing.

The following day Pat heard that Mrs Sutton was ill and that her daughter had called the doctor. Pat went over to see her and found her sitting in front of the fire, wearing a fur coat. She was desperately cold, her feet particularly so. Pat ran back to her own house and rummaged in Hugh's sock drawer for a warm pair of socks. She brought them over, heated them by the fire, put them on Mrs Sutton's feet and began to rub her feet to get the blood flowing more freely. She helped her into bed and Mrs Sutton begged her,

"Stay with me until the Doctor comes."

While she was waiting, Pat used the time to wash Mrs Sutton's hair and curl it. The old lady began to look better and Pat stayed with her until the doctor arrived.

"So did you think you were going to die?" he asked with a smile. "Well, you're not."

After he had completed his examination, her daughter saw him to the door and he stood talking with her for a few moments.

Meanwhile Mrs Sutton and Pat were also talking. Pat had heard her call from the bedroom and went to the door to see what she wanted.

"Oh Pat, I must have the Saviour!" said the old lady.

"Are you sure, Mrs Sutton?" asked Pat, hardly able to believe what she was hearing. She had wept and prayed for two years for Mrs Sutton to say those words and when she finally heard them, she was so shocked that she hardly believed them.

She felt a bit like Rhoda, who opened the door to Peter after his miraculous escape from prison. She and her friends had been praying for his release but she didn't believe it was him when God answered their prayers.

"Yes," Mrs Sutton replied. She stretched out her hand and continued, "Pat, I must have the Lord for my Saviour. No doctor can tell me when I'm going to die, only the Lord."

Pat clasped her hand warmly and asked if she might bring Hugh over to join them. She agreed and Pat ran to fetch Hugh. She had given no thought to the boys and who would look after them while they were in Mrs Sutton's house but God had it all in hand.

"Hugh! Hugh!" she called out as she shot through the front door.

"What is it?" he shouted back.

"Mrs Sutton wants to get saved and wants us to point her to the Lord!"

Hugh gulped and swallowed hard - it would be his first time to point someone to the Lord.

"Right," he said nervously, "we'll seek the Lord first."

The two of them fell to their knees in front of the settee and called on God to guide them and to give them His word and He answered their prayer. They had just got up from their knees when there was a knock at the door. It was Jimmie Carson. Pat was so pleased to see him that she grabbed hold of his lapel and yanked him into the hall, saying as she did so,

"Jimmie, we have to go and point a soul to the Lord. Look after the boys for us!"

Without giving Jimmie a chance to reply, they ran across the road to do the King's business. Hugh read the Scriptures to the old lady and talked with her and she gave her life to Christ. That night, a Saturday, she went into hospital and the following Saturday she died and went to be with Jesus. Pat had the wonderful privilege of having this confirmed to her in a vision – she saw her neighbour, dressed in the white robes of Heaven and wearing a crown on her head. She was especially pleased to see that the new hairdo Pat had given Mrs Sutton was still intact underneath the crown!

# Chapter 19
# Queen Street

"JIMMIE," PAT ANNOUNCED rather tentatively one day, "I had a rather strange vision during my prayer time the other day and God told me I was to share it with you!"

Jimmie made no response so Pat took that as an invitation to continue.

"I saw a building – a meeting house. I could see the shape of the roof and the double doors leading into it. There were houses on both sides of it and a railing in front of it."

Jimmie listened intently but made no comment – he preferred to go away and ask God about it himself. Pat heard nothing from him until one day when he arrived unannounced at the house.

"Come with me and bring James with you," he said. Pat climbed into the passenger seat of his little mini and held James on her lap. Jimmie fitted his rather bulky frame behind the steering wheel and off they set. He drove into Carrick town and then turned into Queen Street without saying anything to Pat. Eventually he pulled up outside a wooden mission hall.

"Is this your vision?" he asked.

Pat looked in amazement at the hall on her left – it was the very hall she had seen in her vision.

"Yes, Jimmie, that's it," she told him, wondering how she had been able to 'see' a place that she had never seen before in real life. Jimmie said no more, just drove the two of them back to Trailcock Road. All was revealed later, after Jimmie had further enquired of the Lord – he was going to rent this mission hall and hold Holiness meetings there on Thursday evenings.

The meetings began in the autumn of 1973. As Jimmie was already committed to meetings in another place for the first few weeks, he asked Rev John Payton to lead them until he was free to take over. For the next seven years, Pat and Hugh were privileged to attend meetings that would challenge them to live holy lives and would delight and thrill them as they witnessed God at work among them, drawing men and women to Himself.

As they listened to the Word of God being taught each week, they began to realise that beyond the preacher, there was a real God hovering over them. They learnt to keep in step with God and to keep short accounts with Him and with the others in the fellowship. They allowed the Spirit of God to reveal wrong thoughts to them by a loss of peace in their hearts which would only be restored when an apology was made and forgiveness sought. As they continually humbled themselves under the hand of God, He drew closer to them, His heart delighting in their desire to please Him. God poured out His forgiveness and cleansing and they would rise from their knees, rejoicing in the knowledge that their hearts were free and clean once more.

They learnt to wait on God and to their great joy, He was pleased to make His Presence felt among them. Often at the end of a meeting they were unable to move because of the reality of God's Presence. They were learning to walk with God and to know His Spirit in a deep way. What valuable lessons these were for His handmaiden.

Soon more and more people began to attend Queen Street and Jimmie asked a young lady called Liz Lacey to lead the meetings. She was a nurse and God had given her a great burden to see other nurses won for Christ. She encouraged a group of nurses to come by telling them,

"You'll go in one way and come out changed. God is there!"

They were intrigued by what she said and agreed to attend. The five girls all ended up sitting in the front row just opposite the bench that had been placed at the front to serve as a penitent form. Anne Cuthbert, who was one of the nurses, wasn't very impressed as she watched Jimmie preaching.

"Look at that auld fella," she thought. "The perspiration's pouring out of him – his jacket's soaked and his grey hair's standing on end because he keeps scratching it!"

She didn't know of course that Jimmie kept moving his hand over his head as he felt God burden him for the people who were listening to him and she certainly didn't know what would happen at the end of the meeting. When Jimmie finished preaching, he invited his listeners to come out to the penitent form as an indication that God had spoken to them and that they were willing to follow Jesus. As he did so, her friend, Winnie, whispered urgently to her,

"Here girl, we've got to go out to the front."

"Not me," Anne whispered back, "I'm not budging."

She had no intention of making any response and was thinking about what she was going to have for supper when suddenly it seemed as though God Himself lifted her off her seat and threw her down on her knees in front of the penitent form.

Pat was in the meeting too and Jimmie had previously told them that when folks responded to the message, he would walk around the hall and touch the shoulders of those whom he wanted to counsel the enquirers. That night he touched Pat's shoulder and she asked God which person He wanted her to talk to. She felt He pointed out Anne to her and so she led her over to a corner of the room to talk with her privately. She had had no training in counselling so she just relied on the Lord to guide her. As she waited on Him, she was directed to some verses in Isaiah chapter 58.

"If thou turn away thy foot from the Sabbath, from doing thy pleasure on My holy day; and call the Sabbath a delight, the holy of the Lord, honourable; and shalt honour Him, not doing thine own ways, nor finding thine own pleasure, nor speaking thine own words," Pat read softly, "then shalt thou delight thyself in the Lord; and I will cause thee to ride upon the high places of the earth, and feed thee with the heritage of Jacob thy father; for the mouth of the Lord hath spoken it."

Anne listened to the words and began to cry – surely God was speaking right to her heart. She knew without any explanation what God required of her. She had been in a relationship with a doctor, a Sikh and felt that God was asking her to give up this relationship and serve Him. Pat led her in a prayer of repentance and faith and she rose from her knees a new creature in Christ Jesus, determined indeed to delight herself in the Lord, honour Him with her life and follow Him always.

People from all walks of life turned up at the meetings and one evening a group of long-haired young men, dressed in jeans walked up the aisle. They took their seats and listened to Jimmie preaching. After he finished everyone sat in silence, waiting on God and He didn't disappoint. His Holy Spirit descended with such strong conviction of sin that no one could move, despite the fact that it was now midnight. Pat noticed Jimmie pacing up and down the aisle as though he was in some distress. Very quietly, she slipped over to speak to him,

"What's wrong, Brother?" she whispered.

"God has moved on these souls and many need private counselling," he replied.

"Bring them round to our home," Pat suggested.

"I daren't move them for fear the Holy Ghost will leave if they start talking in the cars."

"I don't think you have any other option. We can't stay here any longer," Pat insisted.

With that Jimmie went up into the pulpit and told the people,

"Keep yourselves in the attitude of prayer. Go quietly to your cars and drive round to the Logans' home, go into their living room and continue in prayer. Make no talking either here, in your car or in their home. Keep in prayer for souls as they are counselled to get through to God."

As Pat walked into her living room that night, she was so thankful that she had obeyed His Voice earlier in the day, though she had seen no sense in the instruction she had received,

"I want you to wash the carpet from one end of the living room to the other."

While James was sleeping, she moved all the furniture to one end of the room, got down on her knees with a bucket of water, some Flash, a large sponge and a towel. She washed that area till it smelt sweet and fresh and then repeated the whole process for the other end of the room. Now as she gazed at the men and women who were lying prostrate on her floor, their noses pressed against the carpet, crying out to

God in prayer, she understood the need for her hard work. And as each one was taken out of the room to be counselled in private in another room, returning with the joy of God on their faces, she knew that no labour He could ask of her would be too great.

When the last new convert returned to the living room, the accordion was taken out and they sang their praises in the Presence of the King of Kings – what a wonderful evening! It was well after three o'clock in the morning when they slipped quietly into their cars and drove home.

The following Thursday evening, six short-haired young men, dressed in smart suits, shirts and ties arrived to join the group in the Mission Hall. For a moment or two no one recognised them and wondered who they might be, then folk began to smile as they realised that these were the "hippies" of the previous week, changed on the outside as well as the inside!

## Chapter 20
# In The Battle

JIMMIE FELT THAT God had laid it on his heart to start an Open Air Gospel meeting on the green beside Carrickfergus Castle, so Pat and Hugh and some others assembled there one Sunday afternoon at three o'clock. Jimmie opened the proceedings by leading them on his accordion in some hymn singing. One or two others took part and then Jimmie preached.

Pat had stood rather uncertainly throughout the whole thing – it was her first experience of open air work and she really didn't know what to do. When they met afterwards at her house, Pat expressed her concern to Jimmie.

"It would have been nice if we had known what to do," she said.

Jimmy laughed and replied,

"Seek the Lord, open your mouth and He will fill it."

Suddenly it all became clearer for Pat and some others who had felt the same way. They sought the Lord's face through the week and it was all so different the next time they held the open air meeting. One after another went to the microphone, no longer afraid of it now that God had given them something to do.

Some of them sang, some told their story, some read from the Scriptures and Jimmie preached.

This would be the pattern for Sunday afternoons for the next seven years. Whatever the weather, sun, rain or snow, Jimmie and his helpers met to sing, to preach, to talk to those who gathered and to give out tracts. During the summer months, Carrickfergus, with its fine Norman castle, attracted visitors from all over the world and many of them photographed or filmed the open air meeting as if it too was one of the attractions. Pat often wondered how many people sat in their homes in far-away places and listened to the Gospel and prayed that God would use the footage to draw their hearts out after Him.

Although many people passed by the little group without so much as a glance, there were others who sat on the grass on sunny afternoons and listened to the entire service. Still others sat unnoticed in their cars with the windows wound down. Unknown to Pat or anyone else in the group, one of these regulars was a man who used to bring his eighty-five year old mother to the green every Sunday afternoon because she enjoyed the service so much.

Years later as Pat stood in the meeting, praying for the souls of those within earshot, she noticed one of the group, a lady called Hannah, engrossed in conversation with a gentleman. Hannah called Pat over at the end and introduced her to the man, who shook her hand warmly and proceeded to tell her his story,

"About five years ago, every Sunday afternoon, I used to buy my newspapers and take my elderly mother to Carrickfergus Green. I would park the car in front of the open air meeting so that she could listen to it. It was her treat every Sunday. I never bothered to listen – just relaxed and read my newspapers. Then one Sunday you were out at the microphone and you told a story about a woman who had come to see you in your home. As you talked with her, you found yourself saying to her,

'Do you know what you need? You need Jesus.'

This came across to me as 'YOU need Jesus'. Your voice was loud and distinct."

"The years passed and my mother died. I was a travelling salesman and one dank, miserable night, I found myself in England. I was exhausted and very hungry but everywhere was full and I had to go without a meal. At last I managed to find a Bed and Breakfast. I went into the unwelcoming room, threw off my wet coat and sat on the edge of the bed with my head in my hands. Eventually, I lifted my head and noticed a Gideon Bible on the bedside table. I picked it up and read a few verses. A groan rose up within me and I fell on my knees and cried out to God in my despair."

"Then I heard your voice from that open air meeting, 'YOU need Jesus'. There and then I asked Jesus to forgive me and save me and He did. I returned home and now I'm a Pastor in a church here at home. Every opportunity I get, I share my testimony."

How thankful Pat was that God had called the little group to take the battle into the open air. Should this Pastor be the only person who would ever respond, the years of standing, braving the elements would be worth it.

The battle continued to be fought in the Tuesday night prayer meeting too. The Spirit of God would often place a burden on someone's heart and the others would share the burden. This happened one evening when God laid a burden on Sammy Tully's heart for his father. Although he professed to be saved, Sammy was given such a burden for him that he realised he wasn't saved and began to cry out to God on his behalf. As they prayed, some pleaded and battled for his soul while others began to praise God for what He was doing. The Presence of the Lord came down so powerfully that Pat thought the bungalow roof would be lifted off.

In the middle of the prayer time, the phone rang – it was an amazing answer to their prayer. Sammy's father had been fast asleep in bed but was awakened by such a sense of conviction that he had fallen out of bed onto his knees and surrendered his life to Jesus.

On other occasions, Pat and Hugh went into battle on their own. One evening they received a frantic phone call from Hannah, the mother of Heather, one of the nurses who attended the prayer meetings.

"Pat, please pray!" she cried down the phone. "One of my close friend's relatives has been rushed into hospital. She has taken an overdose."

Hannah and her husband Ernie had followed the ambulance into the hospital and Hannah reported that the young girl was in intensive care, very seriously ill. The doctors did not hold out much hope for her. Everyone was frantic with worry and didn't know what to do.

Hannah knew that the only thing they could do was to pray but they were all too upset and worried to pray – they needed someone to intercede for them. Hannah thought of Pat and Hugh though she didn't know them well enough to have their phone number. Not to be deterred, however, she called the operator, who was very helpful and eventually was able to give her the number she needed.

Pat and Hugh immediately promised to pray and the two of them battled through the night, pleading for her life and her soul. Hannah rang twice during the night to give them the latest news. In the early hours of the morning, Pat and Hugh sensed that the battle had been won and began to praise God for His mercy. As they were doing so, the phone rang – the news was good – the girl was showing signs of recovery! Hannah was amazed when Pat told her they already knew because God had told them!

At the very heart of the battle they were engaged in was the strong desire to see God move in Revival as He had in the past. They encouraged others to join them in the battle, including Hannah's daughter, Heather. She had become a Christian through the Nurses Christian Fellowship in Whiteabbey Hospital and had become firm friends with Pat's friend, Liz. After about eighteen months, she became discontented with the quality of her Christian life. She began to realise that there was much more to it than just being saved. She wanted to know more about the power of the Holy Spirit in her life. She had read the stories of the great servants of God like Brainard, Hudson Taylor and McCheyne and knew that she was not living as they had lived. The Holy Spirit was creating a hunger in her soul and she began to realise that it would cost to go deeper with Him. She was willing for this but didn't know how to go about it.

During one of the services in Abbotts Cross Church, she found that she could not join in singing the hymn 'It is well with my soul' and really mean it. This upset her greatly and on realising this, Liz introduced her to Jimmie. She was whisked off by car to the Logan house where she met Pat and Hugh. This marked the beginning of a period in her life that she would later describe in this way:

"They were years of teaching from the Word of God; years of prayer and growing in grace; years of sweet, sweet fellowship with God's chosen people, who were prepared to follow Jesus and sacrifice much to gain knowledge of Him and to do His will. When I look back, I often wonder in amazement how I was privileged to be in such company and sincerely feel my unworthiness very acutely. God took a group of people who for a very short time were connected – He then took them to other places on individual journeys before bringing all things together in His time and purpose in Revival. The one link throughout all the strands was Spirit-filled prayer. The end is not yet. True Revival only comes when God has a people who have lived for Him and can prove that in every circumstance of life, Jesus is Lord. That takes years in the making – people who have overcome."

Being in the front line of the battle was an exhausting business and after a while, Jimmie sensed that they should have a praise meeting once a month to give them a time of release from the battle. These were wonderful evenings of praise and their hearts were refreshed and renewed by the praise and the reading of God's Word. One such evening was particularly refreshing for Pat. She had spent the afternoon getting the room ready and baking for the supper and was more than a little tired. She felt a bit like Martha, busy about many things. All too soon, the meeting was almost over and Jimmie called for a time of prayer during which they would thank God for meeting with them.

Pat listened as one after another thanked God for meeting them and she began to feel cheated for she could not truthfully say that God had met with her in any real sense. So, being Pat, she told God so. She was the last to pray and she thanked God for meeting with her brothers and sisters, then added,

"But You haven't met with me Lord."

She tried to continue her prayer but something strange happened – the Holy Spirit came on her and she began to laugh and laugh – wonderful, refreshing, releasing Holy Spirit inspired laughter. The laughter spread around the room. They had never experienced anything like that before but recognised it as a precious gift from God – one of the most refreshing pleasures God can give His children. How thankful Pat was that she had been honest in her prayer – she would not have missed those moments for anything. It made the battle bearable.

## Chapter 21
## Here for a Reason

PAT AND JAMES walked across the playground. It was hard to believe that the years had passed so quickly – it was James' first day at school –no longer a baby but a little man stepping out proudly with his schoolbag on his back. A young woman came towards them and at first Pat didn't recognise her.

"It's one of the Hill girls – but which one?" thought Pat. "I haven't seen any of them for years."

As they greeted each other, Pat realised that it was Anne. The memories of her mother came flooding back. She had invited Mrs Hill to a prayer meeting in Pat's mother's home some time ago and after that meeting, Mrs Hill had gone home, knelt down in her kitchen and given her heart to the Lord. She had recently become seriously ill with cancer of the lungs and Pat guessed that Anne had come home to relieve her sister, Ellen, who had been nursing their mother. As they talked, Pat sensed the Spirit of God speaking into her heart and she spoke out what He had been saying,

"Anne, you are here for a reason."

Anne's reply was very matter-of-fact,

"Yes, to look after Mummy."

Pat knew that their meeting was significant and began to pray for Anne's salvation. They met up each day at the school gate and on the Wednesday, Pat knew that she was to invite her to a mission which was being held by Rev Sam Workman in a hall nearby. Anne agreed to go and that night Rev Workman had the joy of leading her to the Lord at the end of the meeting. She then told him about her Mum and he decided to accompany Anne and Pat to Mrs Hill's home, where Anne shared her exciting news. Mrs Hill was just delighted.

Later that evening, Anne rang her husband in England with her news. Although she wasn't sure how he would react, she couldn't contain her joy as she told him what had happened. To her amazement, he responded by crying out to God for salvation while she was still on the phone with him. What a day! When Pat heard this new development, she reminded Anne of what she had said to her when they first met,

"That's what I meant when I said that you were here for a reason!"

The following morning, Pat met Anne at the school and her sister, Ellen, was with her.

"Did you hear Anne's good news, Ellen?" Pat asked and Ellen looked at Anne, whose face was just shining.

"I got saved last night at the Mission," Anne announced.

"Anne, that's alright if that's what you want but it's not for me."

Once again, Pat sensed the Spirit within her speak and she spoke out before she really thought about how her words might sound,

"Ellen, you don't know what God will have to do to bring you to Himself."

Mrs Hill passed away not long after that encounter and Pat went to bring some comfort to the Hill family, accompanied by Nessie Campbell, a fellow worker and one of Pat's neighbours. Before they left the home that night, they had pointed another sister, Davina, to the Lord. As they walked out of the dining room into the hall, they met Ellen.

"Davina has just sought the Lord," said Pat. Ellen's reply was filled with anger,

"He got my Mummy but He won't get me!"

One morning, five weeks later, Pat asked God to bless her through His Word and He gave her Luke chapter 15, which contains the story of the parable of the lost sheep. Although Pat thanked God for His Word to her, she had to be honest and confess that she hadn't really experienced the blessing she had asked for! Just then, the phone rang – it was Anne Hill, phoning from her home in England, screaming down the line,

"Patsy, Samuel's dead!"

Samuel was Anne's youngest brother, a young man in his twenties. Pat couldn't believe what she was hearing – only the night before, Hugh had been visiting in the Hills' home and Samuel had popped his head around the door to say goodnight to him. That was the last time he was seen alive. Anne felt so helpless, living so far away and so pleaded with Pat,

"Please go down to Daddy's and see if Ellen is alright."

Pat assured her that she would and immediately rang Hugh. They went together to the family home where four or five others had gathered. Pat asked the Lord for His direction and He told her to go over to Ellen.

"Anne phoned me," Pat began, "she is really concerned about you. She wants you to ring her."

"I'll have to go to my house. Daddy doesn't have a phone," Ellen said through her tears. Pat offered to go with her and Ellen accepted. On the way Pat asked her if she had ever thought about getting saved.

"All the time," was the surprising reply.

"I've been attending the Gospel Hall," she explained.

By this time they had arrived at Ellen's home and once they were inside, Pat turned to ask her,

"Ellen, would you like to get saved?"

"Yes I would," was the firm reply.

"Do you have a Bible?" Pat asked.

Ellen brought a huge Bible over to where Pat was standing. It was open at the place where Ellen had been reading the previous night and Pat was astonished to see that it was the very passage the Lord had given Pat earlier that day. The two women knelt down in the hallway and Pat used the story of the Lost Sheep to point Ellen to the Lord. When they rose from their knees, Ellen phoned her sister Anne to tell her what had happened. Despite their intense grief at the sudden loss of their brother, there was also rejoicing in their conversation and a great sense of peace in the midst of their sorrow.

As Pat and Ellen walked back to the Hills' house, Ellen told her what had happened earlier in the day. Their other brother, William, had called at the house, gone upstairs and found Samuel lying dead in bed. What a shock! He had called out to Ellen, who had been downstairs at the time. She had not wanted to go upstairs but very reluctantly did so at her brother's insistence. She stood at the bottom of her brother's bed and in that moment of shock and distress, heard God speak to her with great clarity,

"Where would your soul be if it was you lying in that bed?"

She could only say, as the reality of it all shook her to the core of her being,

"Lost in hell forever!"

Once again God had placed His handmaiden in the right place at the right time and given her the right words to say in order to draw another soul into His Kingdom. Although she grieved over the circumstances that it had taken for Ellen to respond to God's call on her life, she couldn't help but rejoice at her salvation.

Chapter 22
# Navy Stilettos or God's Anointing?

"WOULD YOU SING at our wedding?"

Pat turned round quickly to see who had tapped her on the shoulder and made the request. It was Liz, who had met her husband-to-be in the meetings at Queen Street.

Pat began to smile,

"What kept you?" she asked, "The Lord told me weeks ago that I was to sing at your wedding and even told me what hymn I was to sing!"

Although choosing the hymn had not been a problem, choosing something to wear most certainly would be. Times were difficult financially and some of the people who lived nearby were having to sell their homes and move to rented accommodation. How thankful Pat and Hugh were for the way God had provided their home and for the way He had enabled them to stay there. They managed to cut the grocery bill and wore second hand clothes – Pat was amazed and pleased to discover that the Lord made sure the clothes weren't too out of fashion! Clothes suitable for a wedding would not be so easy to come by.

So Pat was greatly relieved when, close to the wedding date, Hugh's mum gave her a skirt in an unusual tartan, a matching waistcoat with fancy brass buttons and a grey cotton long-sleeved blouse. Liz loaned her a floppy navy blue picture hat and a navy bag – the outfit was almost complete. Just the shoes to choose and she was finished. Pat went to her wardrobe and lined up her three pairs of shoes. She looked at the navy stilettos, the black court shoes and the black patent sling-backs with low heels that were in need of repair.

"Now Lord," she enquired, "which do You want me to wear?"

All her training in window dressing and fashion pointed to the navy stilettos as the only possible choice but her obedient heart left the choice with the Lord. She couldn't help adding,

"Lord, those navy shoes are the only ones that will go with everything!"

"Not for My Glory," came the reply. She asked about the black court shoes and the reply was the same. That only left the patent pump shoes.

"But they need to be mended, Lord."

"Get them mended," His Voice came clearly.

"For My Glory," He told her. Pat had thought the Lord's choice might turn out to be this pair but made a last protest,

"Black patent with a navy blue picture hat – oh no!"

"Do you want to go into the pulpit without My anointing or do you want My anointing to sing at the wedding?" the Lord asked. There was no further protest.

"Lord, You know I need You. I'll obey."

On the day of the wedding Pat dressed in her outfit, took a last longing look at the navy stilettos and placed the newly mended black sling-backs on her feet. She enjoyed the wedding service and sang the song the Lord had given her. Afterwards she and Hugh walked around the beautiful grounds of the hotel where the reception had been held.

Suddenly Pat looked up to see a cine camera pointing at her. Oh no – not only did she have to wear shoes that didn't match but now the fact would be recorded for posterity! Although the smile stayed on her face when she realised that it was the minister's wife who was taking the footage, inside she was squirming with embarrassment. She knew, of course what God was doing – stripping her of all the vanity associated with fashion and weddings in His desire to make her more Christ-like.

Some weeks later she understood just why her complete obedience had been so necessary. One of the bride's friends, a nurse from Whiteabbey Hospital, had popped in to the church to see the wedding. She had heard Pat singing her song and told Liz later on,

"I stood listening to the singing. I didn't hear one word that she sang but I was so gripped by God that I got saved on the spot."

The singing had also touched the heart of a second girl and as a result, she too got saved some days later. God's anointing had been on the song and on the singer. Would this have been the case if the shoes had been navy stilettos? Pat would never know the answer to that question but in her heart she believed that there was a close connection between her obedience to the will of God and the anointing of God on her service for Him. She felt that it had been necessary for her to become a fool for Christ that day, to count her appearance as nothing and to allow God to work in the deep places of her life, stripping away what didn't please Him.

It was one of many similar 'strippings' that Pat had experienced over the previous years, until God was sure that His handmaiden would obey instantly, without question and without hesitation, that her only concern would be for 'His Glory'. Into that obedient heart He was then able to pour His compassion and a strong sense of identification with the needs of others.

Chapter 23
# All For His Glory

ELLEN'S CONVERSION USHERED in a new chapter in Pat's ministry among the many pensioners who lived in the area. God had given Pat a vision about this work and Ellen also felt a call to it so they agreed to go out together, following the example set by Jesus when He sent out His disciples in twos. They prayed much about how they would proceed and decided to visit eight homes each week and bring tracts to give to those who would accept them. The first bungalow they visited was the one Pat had seen in her vision and the occupiers, Mr and Mrs McFarland, made them very welcome and listened intently as Ellen and Pat shared the Gospel with them. They were happy for the two ladies (or 'girls' as they called them!) to include them in their weekly visits and so began a friendship that resulted in Pat and Ellen feeling like part of their family.

They visited other pensioners too, listening to their problems, praying with them and in many cases, leading them to Christ. Everything they did was for His Glory alone and God honoured their passion for Him by using them to touch many lives with His love and compassion. Often they found themselves visiting the hospitals where these elderly people would eventually die, bringing comfort as well as the challenge of the Gospel.

When Mr McFarland became ill, he was taken to Whiteabbey Hospital. Ellen and Pat met to pray for him and God spoke to them as they were on their knees, interceding for him.

"Get up and go to see his wife and offer her a lift to the hospital," was the direction they were given.

Mrs McFarland was delighted with their offer and soon all three of them were on the way in to the ward. Her husband waved them over with some urgency and the ladies could see that he appeared to be troubled. As they chatted they discovered that he had been visited earlier on that day by his minister. During the previous few days, he had been under great conviction of sin but his request to his minister to point him to the Lord was met with a pat on his back and the words,

"You're not too bad and you're not too good, so don't worry, you're alright for Heaven."

Mr McFarland knew that he wasn't 'alright for Heaven' and so was overjoyed to see 'the girls' arrive with his wife.

"Pray with me, I want to get saved," he pleaded with them. When his wife heard his request, she plonked herself down on the bed –

"Me too!" she announced.

Pat and Ellen wasted no time in leading them both to Jesus and then the four of them talked and laughed together at the bedside, giving all the glory to God.

Although Pat and Ellen became close friends, they hardly ever visited each other socially – there was really no time for socialising, such was their desire to please God by helping others to find Jesus and walk in His ways. So Pat was rather surprised by God's instruction to her one morning during her quiet time,

"Get up off your knees and go and visit Ellen."

She got ready and was soon on her way up Victoria Road where Ellen lived. As she came to a place where she could see the pensioners' bungalows, she heard His Voice again,

"Go and see Mrs McFarland."

"But Lord, You told me to go and visit Ellen," she began to protest but quickly remembered that it was better to obey His Voice.

"You know best, Lord," she whispered and crossed the road to Mrs McFarland's house. As she walked up the path, she realised that there was a key in the lock and then noticed that the door was slightly open. Pat knocked the door, called out Mrs McFarland's name and then gently pushed open the door. As she entered the hallway, she heard a groan and rushed into the living room, where she found Mrs McFarland alone and in some distress. Pat laid her hands on the old lady's head and prayed that God would touch her and heal her. As she finished praying, the nurse, who called to check on her every day, came into the room and took over.

"My dear, you have saved her life," she told Pat. "She was having a heart attack."

As usual, Pat was careful to give God the glory –

"We have only the Lord to thank – He sent me."

On one of their weekly visits to the pensioners' bungalows, a rather disgruntled gentleman answered the door and greeted them with an abrupt, "Yes?" He listened to what they had to say but Pat and Ellen both felt that he had no interest whatsoever in the Gospel. Just before they left, however, he mentioned his wife, who was ill in Whiteabbey Hospital and asked them if they would go to see her. They agreed to do so and set out in Ellen's old car.

At that time, Ellen drove an old banger which just drank water by the gallon and sure enough, halfway along their journey, they had to pull in to give the car a 'drink'. By then they were beginning to run out of time, as they had to be back in Carrick to pick up children before the end of the school day, so they set out again, praying for the rest of the journey.

At last they pulled into the hospital and followed the gentleman's directions to his wife's ward. A nurse was with her and they recognised her as Margaret Collins, a lady who attended the Queen Street Fellowship. She slipped away quietly, sensing that Pat and Ellen had come to talk about spiritual things. They told the lady what had happened that morning and how her husband had suggested their visit. They spoke to her about Jesus and were delighted to hear her ask them,

"How can I get saved?"

The whole thing had only taken a few minutes and Pat and Ellen felt that God had already prepared her heart. Margaret returned to the bedside and the lady's toenails finally got attended to! She was followed by the lady's husband who couldn't help but notice the joy on his wife's face as she told him that she had got saved. She had no Bible but Ellen was more than happy to leave her small Bible with her. The lady died not long afterwards.

Time after time Pat discovered that if she obeyed the Voice of the Lord in her heart and served Him with a humble heart, giving all the glory to Him, He brought many people to Himself. She recognised more easily now the Voice she had first heard in a laburnum tree as a young unhappy girl in London. She often found herself smiling and even marvelling at the ways and the people God would use to pass on His Word to others. On one occasion, He used a lovely young Japanese lady who had attended the prayer meetings in their home and also the Queen Street meetings. She very kindly offered to babysit for Pat and Hugh to let them attend a meeting. Although it was quite late when they returned, Atsiko had kept the boys up and they were so excited about what Atsiko had taught them that evening. It was close to Christmas and she had shown them how to make Japanese birds out of Christmas paper to hang as decorations on the Christmas tree.

"And we can sing in Japanese!" they announced.

Pat and Hugh were very impressed as they listened to their boys singing "I Have the Love of Jesus Deep in my Heart" in Japanese.

When the time came for Atsiko to return home, some of the ladies at the prayer meeting gave her a cuddly toy – a large white lamb – to remind her of Ireland and the lambs she had seen for the first time in her life. Seeing those lambs had helped her to understand more clearly the whole concept of Jesus as the Lamb of God. She too had gifts for her friends and gave Pat a green silk bookmark on which a Scripture text had been written in gold, in Japanese, of course! She had taken the trouble to write out the verse in English and wrapped that around the bookmark.

Next morning, Pat and Ellen set out on their visitation. They prayed about where to go and sensed that God would have them visit a lady who was dying, so they set out for Whiteabbey Hospital. Anne Cuthbert, one of their friends who worked there had been greatly burdened for her and often prayed for her and wept for her. As they hurried along, they asked God to give them His Word and Ellen heard Him whisper a verse in her heart. Pat opened her Bible to look for the verse Ellen had been given and she saw the bookmark. She took it out to show Ellen, who glanced at it and then started to laugh,

"Patsy, that's the text we've been looking for!"

"Doesn't the Lord have a great sense of humour," Pat thought, "and a great sense of timing!"

They hurried into the ward where the lady was lying but were disappointed when a nurse told them,

"It's not possible for you to speak to her, she's sedated."

The two women took a seat in the corridor and began to pray. The Lord told them to go in anyway so they walked on in and sat at her bedside. They told her who they were and why they had come and began to tell her about Jesus. Then Pat said,

"It's time to read the promise God gave you for her this morning."

Ellen opened her Bible at Matthew chapter 28, verse 3 and read the lovely words,

"Come unto me all ye who labour and are heavy laden and I will give you rest."

Pat noticed the lady's countenance change as she brightened up and with a look of determination said,

"I want to get saved."

What joy they knew as they pointed her to Jesus and saw her face shine with the joy of the Lord. They couldn't stay long because the children had to be picked up from school but they heard from Anne later that when she visited her, she was glowing on the outside and on the inside! They rejoiced as they thought of the way God had used four of His handmaidens, one from the other side of the world, to bring new life to an old lady. How wonderful to realise that her death, a few days later, was merely the transition from life on earth to eternal life in Heaven.

In these years, God was also using Hugh for His Glory. He gave him a burden for the people living near them in the Orlits. Hugh had already been witnessing in hospitals and pubs but felt that God was calling him to preach in this new area. This was difficult for Hugh as he was a quiet man by nature but, like Pat, he was determined to be obedient so he set aside Wednesday evenings for this work. He brought tracts with him and handed them out when he had finished preaching. Meanwhile, Pat would remain at the house and spend the time praying for God's blessing on his ministry. God did bless and at least four people became Christians as a result of his faithfulness. He became known as the 'Preacher man' and one young man became so convicted of his sin that one evening he ended up on his knees, crying out to God to bring the Preacher man along to his house. He looked up and there was Hugh walking past his window. He followed Hugh home and Hugh led him to the Lord.

The following year, Hugh felt called to stand alone in the Market Place in Carrickfergus and preach. Once again Pat supported him by praying at home but during the third year, God directed her to go with him. In later years, others joined them.

Every so often in the Queen Street meetings, an open night would be held when those who attended were free to bring something to the meeting that God had laid on their hearts. One afternoon in 1980 Pat felt that God was leading her to sing a hymn that reminded her of her mother, who used to sing it on Sunday mornings as she and Pat stood together in the kitchen in London, making breakfast for the family. The hymn was 'Sweet is the Promise, I will not Forget Thee' and as she sat in Queen Street that evening, sensing the nudge of the Holy Spirit to sing it, Pat remembered how the tears had come to her eyes when it had been sung in church the Sunday after she had become a Christian.

"Father," she whispered, "You know how this hymn always makes me weep when I think of my mother singing it all those years ago."

The prompting of the Spirit only got stronger, however, so she made her way up to the pulpit. She led the people in that great hymn and they responded with vigour, singing with all their hearts. As Pat looked down at all her friends sitting in the congregation, she sensed God reveal something of His heart for them and she began to speak out what He was saying. The tears came to her eyes as she shared her sense that the work in Queen Street was going to close soon and that God would call many of those listening to her into other work for Him, both at home and abroad.

"We needed to sing this hymn tonight," she concluded, "so that you will always remember how great He is and know that He will never forget you or leave you."

Over the next few years, Pat saw God do what He had revealed to His handmaiden as one by one many in the group were called to different places – Taiwan, Papua New Guinea, India and Japan. Others were called into ministry in various parts of Great Britain while those who stayed at home continued to serve the King and bring Glory to His name.

Chapter 24
# Testing Times

BEING THE LORD'S handmaiden and living a life of obedience and holiness does not of course mean that everything will move along smoothly. On the contrary, those who seek to follow the Lord closely find that faith gets tested and the enemy tries very hard to destroy any work for God that is attempted. Often there are dark periods where attacks seem to come from all sides and the time following the closure of the work in Queen Street was one such time for Pat and Hugh.

Pat had gone out to visit some folks who had been bereaved and when she returned home, young James ran to greet her but in his excitement, he knocked her off her feet. She knew from the excruciating pain she felt as she lay helpless that some damage had been done. In the days and weeks that followed she rested as best as she could with three lively boys in the house but the pain remained and if anything, got worse. Jimmie asked Rev Workman to pray with her but forgot to tell him to walk right in. Pat had to crawl to the door to let him in as she couldn't pull herself upright!

As one week had rolled into the next with no improvement, Hugh had done what he could to look after the boys and Pat's friends, Anne, Liz and Ellen had all rallied round to help with washing Pat's hair, washing clothes and other jobs. As Christmas approached, Pat had cried out to God to at least be able to sit in a chair for Christmas – she had begun to feel that she would never walk again.

While he chatted to her, Rev Workman mentioned that a man called Bobby McGregor had helped his wife when she had a back problem and urged her to try to see him. Hugh wasted no time and tried to get an appointment with Bobby McGregor, but he was a very busy man and at first told Hugh that he wouldn't be able to see Pat for some time.

"But my wife can't walk!" Hugh protested, "Something has to be done!"

The desperate tone in his voice must have struck a chord because Hugh was told to bring Pat in and he would try to fit her in. When he examined her, he said that she had damaged three discs in her back and one of them was the worst possible disc to injure – no wonder she had been in such pain. He treated her and gave her an appointment for a week later, which was not his usual practice. Little by little the treatments and the rest began to work and she was able to sit in a chair at Christmas time, as she had longed to do but it was three long months before she felt better.

In the middle of all of that, Hugh began to realise that he would probably soon be made redundant from his job with ICI. He was still only in his late forties and his friends all assured him that he would soon find another job, so he began the soul-destroying task of filling in application forms and writing letters to other firms. It was all to no avail and letter after letter dropped through the letter-box, all carrying the same message –'Sorry, we regret to inform you that your application has not been successful'.

Eventually the day he had dreaded arrived and their future looked rather bleak. The small amount of redundancy money was used to do up the house and they looked for creative ways to save money. Pat patched clothes rather than discarding them, cut down on groceries and rationed chocolate biscuits to once a week. Anne and other good friends passed on clothes to Pat who used a little sewing magic to change them and make them look fashionable. Others were selling their homes and moving into rented accommodation but God encouraged them to hold on to their little bungalow and assured them that, as always, He would be their Provider. Despite all of these efforts, they were only just getting by.

They even wondered if the Lord would have them emigrate. Pat's brother, Noel, had already moved to Canada and was very happy to write a letter offering to sponsor them to move too. They also sent for brochures about Australia and were greatly impressed by the beautiful homes out there. All of this was taken to the Lord for, above anything else, they wanted to do His will. Neither Pat nor Hugh received any guidance to move so they just accepted that they were to stay in Carrickfergus.

In July of 1981, they received a call to say that their friend and mentor, Jimmie Carson, had died from a heart attack. He had suffered from angina for a long time but never let it hold him back from serving the King and spreading His Gospel at every opportunity. Their hearts were heavy as they mourned for their friend and attended his funeral. At the graveside, Pat stood beside Mabel Shaw, who was Rev Shaw's wife and also a relative of Jimmie's and the two ladies agreed that Jimmie would have thoroughly enjoyed the hearty singing both in the service and at the graveside. Jimmie's death and the closing down of the Queen Street work left a gap in their lives and they sometimes wondered what God had in store for them.

They were being tested too in their family life. The boys were much loved and prayed for and at the beginning seemed to really enjoy all the meetings and the singing that went on in their home. When Richard was ten years old, he even felt that God was calling him to work in Brazil, maybe as an engineer. Things changed, however, as they entered their teens. Both Richard and Jonathan passed the eleven plus examination and attended Carrickfergus Grammar School. Gradually, among the new friends they made, they became embarrassed about religion. Richard got interested in punk rock music and was persuaded to try smoking in an attempt to appear 'cool'.

The first Pat knew anything of his changing attitudes was one evening when he was about fifteen. He was supposed to be drying dishes but instead flung the drying cloth on the floor and announced,

"I'm away out!"

He stormed off to a nearby friend's house, leaving Pat wondering where her helpful and polite little boy had gone!

For the next few years, Richard continued to attend church with his parents but was keenly aware of the tension between what his parents wanted for him and what he wanted to do with his own life. One Sunday morning, tired after a late night at a disco, his response to Pat's attempts to waken him to go to church was curt and to the point,

"I don't want to go anymore. I won't be going anymore."

Jonathan followed much the same pattern as did James in the years to come and a heartbroken Pat just had to leave them to the Lord and continue to love them and pray for them. She knew that God had His own plans for the boys' lives and she also knew her God well enough to be certain that she could trust Him with her sons.

They were aware, of course, that when their parents prayed, things happened and this was forcefully brought home to them in the summer holidays of 1985. James, who was thirteen at the time, had become good friends with a young boy called Harry Blair, who lived nearby. Pat and Hugh had started praying for them when the boys got friendly. They felt that God had put this family on their hearts and often could be found weeping for their souls.

One day in July, James came rushing into the house, where Pat was serving lunch. His face was ashen and his voice trembled when he tried to tell them what he had heard. On the night of the 11th, Harry had tried to cross the railway line to get to the beach but had not realised that a train was coming. He had been unable to jump out of the way and the train had hit him.

"He's in the Royal Hospital," James cried, "and he needed forty pints of blood!"

Pat sensed the Spirit of God rise up within her.

"Hugh, you serve the rest of the lunch," she murmured, handing him the ladle and dish, "I'm going to pray."

She ran to the bedroom, tears streaming from her eyes, and fell on to her knees beside the bed.

"Oh God, oh God!" she cried, groaning in the depths of her spirit on behalf of this young life. Somehow she knew she had touched the heart of God and felt her body go limp. Then the Voice she knew so well spoke:

"I have heard your cries, the lad shall live and walk with a limp."

As she listened to His words, she also had a picture of young Harry walking with a limp and she was encouraged to see that it didn't look at all awkward but actually seemed quite natural. Pat returned to the table, still shaking from her labours in the Presence of the Almighty God.

Some time later, his mother, Bridie, arrived at the door. She was tired and weary after waiting at Harry's bedside.

"I'm sorry for disturbing you all," she began, "but Harry insisted that I would call with you and ask you to pray for him. He made me promise."

Pat was delighted to be able to tell her that prayer had already been made and shared with her what she had heard God say. Although Bridie made little comment at the time, she and her husband Wesley rejoiced when God's Word came to pass and their son returned home from hospital – alive, but walking with a limp!

## Chapter 25
# Obeying The Voice

GOD DIDN'T ALWAYS speak to Pat at a convenient moment, sometimes choosing to waken her up in the middle of the night. When this happened one night a few years later and Pat heard Him tell her to get up and pray, she groaned and protested,

"Oh Lord, I'm so tired I can't open my eyes. Lord meet me halfway. Let me lie on a minute or two, then draw me to the surface and open my eyes, please."

She drifted back to sleep but a short time later, her eyes opened and she shot out of bed. She didn't want to waken Hugh so she just slipped on a dressing gown and crept along to the living room, where she sat and waited for God to speak. It was four o'clock in the morning.

She didn't have to wait long before she recognised the Voice that she had first heard in the laburnum tree all those years ago.

"Pat, I want you and Hugh to go to Antrim later today before 12 noon, to the Nursing Home where Mrs Duncan is and point her to the Lord. On your way, call in first with June for her approval."

June was Hugh's sister-in-law and Mrs Duncan was her mother. She was an elderly lady who had been in a nursing home for some time. Pat sensed that her time to find Christ had come, so she spent a long time in the quiet darkness, praying for her salvation and binding those powers that would battle against her taking this step.

Over breakfast she shared what God had said with Hugh and the two of them set out for June and David's house. They had been on holiday and were keen to show Pat and Hugh their holiday snaps. Although they were happy to admire the photographs, Pat became anxious that they might miss the time appointed by the Lord.

"We have to be there before twelve, before Mrs Duncan has her lunch," she kept thinking.

They spent a little time explaining to June what they wanted to do and she listened carefully and was happy for them to visit her mother. As they were leaving, she rang the nursing home to say that they were on their way. Everything seemed to be conspiring against them, however, for they got held up in traffic near Antrim.

"We may do this another day," said Hugh as he realised that it was now five to twelve.

"No," was Pat's firm response, "the Lord said today."

They arrived soon afterwards and were warmly greeted at Reception and then brought to where Mrs Duncan was having her hair done. She was delighted to see them and a young assistant informed them,

"We have a nice room in here, where you will get privacy to talk."

The room she showed them was bright and airy and the door had a glass pane in it. Mrs Duncan sat down with Pat and Hugh on either side of her. Pat could see the door from where she was seated. They chatted for a moment or two and then they began to speak about Jesus. Eventually Hugh asked her if she had ever thought about getting saved.

"Many's a time," she told them.

They talked a little more and then Pat asked her,

"Mrs Duncan, would you like Hugh to point you to Jesus now?"

She looked steadily at Pat and replied, "Yes, I would."

Hugh opened his Bible and began to read some Scriptures to her. As he did so, there was a loud banging on the door. Pat looked up and saw a nun standing at the door, indicating that she wanted them to leave the room. For a moment Pat wasn't sure what to do – usually in circumstances like that, she would have gone to the door to see what the lady wanted but she knew that Mrs Duncan was on the very verge of giving her life to the Lord. Just then, the Lord's Voice came to her clearly,

"Pay no attention, keep praying for Mrs Duncan to come to Me."

Pat did her best to ignore the knocking on the door and focused on praying for the lady sitting between them. Eventually the nun gave up and left.

A few moments later, Mrs Duncan prayed for forgiveness and passed from death into life. She looked up at them, her face shining with joy and Pat knew that in Heaven, the angels were singing once again. They hugged their new sister in the Lord, so grateful that the enemy hadn't been able to ruin that special moment by distracting them from their important task. They walked down the hall arm in arm with Mrs Duncan and just before taking their leave of her, Pat whispered in her ear,

"If we don't see you again here, we'll see you up there . . . . ." and she pointed to Heaven, " . . . . . in the Glory."

Mrs Duncan was still smiling broadly as one of the staff appeared to take her to lunch – God's timing had, as usual, been perfect!

By this time, Pat and Hugh had learned the value of always waiting to hear the Voice of God, no matter what the circumstances. So, when someone asked them to speak to the father of Harry Blair, James' friend, their response was to ask God and wait for His prompting. They knelt by the settee and after calling on God for guidance, He gave them a Scripture and told them to go.

When they arrived at the Blairs' house, Wesley seemed to be sleeping. Hugh sat beside him and began to talk to him about spiritual matters but got no response. His eyes remained firmly closed. Then Pat whispered to Hugh,

"Read the Word God gave to you."

"If thou shalt confess with thy mouth the Lord Jesus," Hugh read quietly, "and shalt believe in thine heart that God hath raised him from the dead, thou shalt be saved."

Suddenly Wesley's eyes flew open and there was a broad smile on his face as he turned to them and said,

"That's Romans 10 and 9. I learned that at Sunday School."

"What about it then?" asked Hugh. "Would you like to get saved? Would you have me point you to Christ?"

He was willing and the smile stayed on his face as he came to Jesus. How glad Pat was that they had listened for the Voice to speak, giving them the very Word that would break down the barriers. Wesley died five weeks later – seeing face to face the One in whom he had put his trust.

Some years later Pat met his wife, Bridie, while out shopping. They chatted for a while and Bridie shared how hard she was finding the loss of her husband. Pat sympathised with her and before their conversation finished, she talked to her about Jesus. Bridie found it all very difficult to get hold of but was further challenged when her sister phoned her from Canada to say that her husband had got saved. She began to pray to God for salvation but had no peace in her heart, no assurance that the work had been done.

In the end, she decided to visit Pat and share her problem with her. As Pat listened to her story, at the same time she was listening for the Voice inside and before very long, God had put the name Jim McTernaghan into her mind. He had a special ministry, helping Christians who had deep needs.

"Leave it with me," she told Bridie, "I'll be in touch very soon again."

Bridie was happy to do so and once she had left, Pat sought God's leading again and was directed to phone Jim. He too asked God for guidance and when he phoned Pat back, they arranged to meet with Bridie the next night in her own home. Another Christian lady joined them to pray with Pat while Jim would talk to Bridie.

They were given a warm welcome and Pat was immediately conscious of the Presence of the Lord as they began to talk. Jim prayed and then spent sometime in deep discussion with Bridie about her situation. Pat soon realised why God had guided her to invite Jim to minister into this lady's life – his kind, gentle approach and great patience was just what she needed. Many times she would say that she believed she was a Christian and then Jim would patiently remind her that she still had no peace or assurance. He would read the Bible and Pat and her friend would silently pray for God's power to fall on her and set her free.

Suddenly she cried out in great distress, "I'm not saved! I'm not saved!"

The tears flowed down her cheeks as Jim tenderly led her to the Lord. When she lifted up her head, they could see that her face was shining just the way her husband's had shone when he trusted Jesus. Peace and assurance had come to her heart. The next day Bridie spoke about Jesus to a girl at the petrol station and was amazed to find that the girl listened intently to what she had to say – God's Spirit confirming to her that He was living within her.

So many times through her life, Pat had been aware of the Voice of God - sometimes just the merest whisper, the faintest impression but at other times a clear detailed instruction. It amazed and thrilled her that the God of Heaven should choose to communicate His heart to His handmaiden in this way. She had come to depend on hearing His Voice for her ministry to lost souls and knew that the closer she walked with Him and the more intently she listened to Him, the more He would use and bless her.

## Chapter 26
# The Deep, Deep Cry

PAT LISTENED INTENTLY to the tape which Anne Cuthbert had given to her and something within her rose up in response to what she was hearing. The speaker on the tape was a man from Dublin who had been used of God in a work in Southern Ireland, in the city of Cork. While on a preaching tour of Northern Ireland he had invited anyone who had a burden to pray for Revival in Ireland to visit his work. For many years, Pat had sensed this call on her life and she determined to talk to Anne about joining the proposed trip.

Anne was very keen to make the trip but when they found out the arrangements for it, she wasn't able to go. Pat thought no more about it until she and Hugh visited Sally and Eleanor, whom they had met through a prayer meeting Hugh attended in the Church of the Nazarene. They received a warm welcome from the girls and their lovely family and Pat found herself telling her friends about the visit to Cork. Much to her surprise, their faces lit up and they immediately responded,

"Oh we would love to go."

Ellen Hunter joined them and after spending the previous week in prayer for the trip, the four intrepid ladies set out on their grand adventure.

They enjoyed the long journey through Ireland, marvelling at the beauties of God's creation as they drove along in the July sunshine. Eventually they arrived at their destination, a large house near Cork, and were greeted by the men and women who lived and ministered there. They had dinner with about forty others and enjoyed having fellowship with them. These new brothers and sisters in the Lord had a genuine love for God and shared Pat's passion for Revival.

The next four days were days of refreshing for Pat as they worshipped together - sometimes singing, sometimes taking communion from a single chalice and sometimes simply sitting in silence, waiting for God's Presence, for His renewing power, waiting for Revival. At one of their evening meetings Pat once again experienced the Presence of God in a deep way. His Presence was so real that it seemed as though He was absorbing her into His Holy Being.

How glad she was that she had sat at the back of the room – when the meeting ended and everyone else began to chat, she was able to slip out unnoticed. She had no desire to chat – she didn't want anything to break this amazing sense of His nearness. She wanted to be utterly alone with her God - she was in another world, locked in with Him. The words of a hymn she knew became a sweet reality to her:

"Not a sound invades the stillness
Not a form invades the scene
Save the voice of my Beloved
And the Person of my King

Precious, gentle, holy Jesus
Blessed Bridegroom of my heart
In Thy secret, inner chamber
Thou wilt whisper what Thou art.

Wrapt in deep, adoring silence,
Jesus, Lord I dare not move
Lest I lose the smallest saying
Meant to catch the ear of love."

She was desperate to get to her bedroom to be alone with God and to soak up His Presence. Unknown to her, Ellen, with whom she was sharing a room, had already gone to bed. When Pat arrived in the room, she wanted to talk to her but Pat was so caught up in the Presence of God that she couldn't speak. She didn't even take time to undress, just switched out the light and climbed into bed fully clothed! As she pulled the bedclothes over her head, the only explanation she could give to Ellen was to say,

"I am with God."

His Presence remained with her all night and she stayed awake, basking in His love and delighting in His nearness.

Ellen got up before Pat the next morning and set out breakfast for the two of them. As Pat ate, she began to feel rather uncomfortable – she had pain in her stomach but couldn't work out what was wrong. It wasn't until the weeping came that she recognised what was happening – she had experienced weeping like this before and knew that her pain was a spiritual pain, a glimpse into the heart of God for His people. She began to walk around the room in agonising tears. The pains increased in intensity until they felt just like the pains she had experienced when she gave birth to her children.

"I'm carrying the baby of Revival here," she thought, as another searing pain coursed through her body.

By this time others had begun to arrive in the dining room and some of them helped Pat up the stairs to a little room at the top of the house, where they gently laid her on a bed. She lay there, the pains sweeping over her in waves and as they increased in strength, so the cry for Revival rose up in her spirit and increased until she thought her heart would break. She thought she would die unless this child was delivered.

One of the ladies took her hand and tried to comfort her but Pat was not to be comforted. She knew that God had a deep purpose for her distress and soon she sensed that He wanted everyone in that house to know the depths of prayer and agonising tears that would be required before they would see Revival in Ireland or in the world. Then His Voice spoke to her,

"My people ask – show us how to pray for Revival. Every fibre of your being must be brought under My control. Just as you are now, with no thought for yourself, only for the finished product – Revival. All your thoughts are – the baby must be born. Revival must come or I die. Deep calling unto deep – that is what you are experiencing now."

Three of the ladies left the room, leaving the other to stay with Pat, still holding her hand. The pains and the crying continued – the deep, deep cry for Revival. Gradually they subsided, leaving Pat totally exhausted. The three ladies returned and told Pat they had been praying downstairs.

"We had a Word from the Lord – can you confirm it to us?" they asked.

Pat's reply was instant, "For as soon as Zion travailed, she brought forth her children."

"That was the Word God gave us," they told her, their eyes shining with a shared sense that something significant had happened that morning.

The four ladies sang songs of praise on their eight-hour journey back to the North. God had met with them in a very special way and their hearts were full of joy and thanksgiving. Pat was sure that God had touched her so deeply she would never be the same again. She sensed that this call to pray for Revival would keep ringing out in her heart, that it was part of the great purposes God had for His handmaiden. Although Anne was unable to join her on this occasion, she visited the work in Cork on another occasion and was greatly blessed by God as well.

It was shortly after this that Pat felt a change in the way she and Anne were praying. They had been praying together for many years and one special day God had given them a vision that they didn't fully understand at the time. It was of two little girls sitting on a fence in glorious sunshine looking at a field of golden corn. They were in an orchard and the apple trees partially shaded them from the hot sun. It was a warm, balmy day and they were at peace and in harmony with nature. In the vision the Lord spoke to them,

"Go and play, my daughters, in the golden field but when the Father calls, come and pray."

They hopped off the fence and went laughing into the field of corn.

Soon afterwards Anne saw a postcard of two little girls lying peacefully in the sun and posted it to Pat. It reminded both of them of the vision they had seen and the joy it had brought to them. But now it seemed God was saying that the time for playing in the cornfield was over. He called them to intercede as never before – long arduous intercessions that lasted for hours. They often wept as they tramped the Jericho march up and down the length of Pat's living room, storming the enemy's camp, pushing back the forces of darkness, battling against principalities and powers and claiming victory in the name of Jesus. Week after week, God brought people and situations to their minds and they earnestly stood in the gap for them, crying out to God on their behalf. They felt drained and exhausted after these intercessions and often were left with aching bodies but their spirits rejoiced at the sense of victory God gave them each time. They were doing the work God had called them to do.

## Chapter 27
# Heart Attack

HEART TROUBLE RAN in Hugh's family – his father and younger brother, Brian, had both died of heart attacks. So it should not have been a great shock when Hugh took his first attack at the early age of 49. Two years later, he suffered another one, at which time he was put on medication, to be continued for the rest of his life.

Richard, Jonathan and James, all of whom were in their twenties by this time, were so concerned for their father's health, that they clubbed together to send Pat and Hugh on a surprise short break to Scotland. They found an offer from Seacat – a three day trip for £30. So Pat and Hugh packed up the tent and brought the grocery money with them, hoping that would be enough to meet their needs.

They had a wonderful time, exploring the delights of Scotland but towards the end of the trip, Pat noticed that Hugh didn't seem to be in good form.

"Have I done something to cause this?" she wondered but when she asked Hugh, he assured her that everything was fine.

On their final day, a Saturday, they drove into a little town and decided to make a stop to buy baps and scones and a newspaper. Their plan was to rest for a while near the sea, make a cup of tea and then head for the boat home to Ireland. As they turned into the main street, Pat noticed a sign pointing to the hospital.

"Well, we certainly don't want that!" she laughed.

"We certainly don't," Hugh agreed.

After parking the car, Hugh went off in one direction to buy a newspaper, while Pat went to buy the food. As she returned, she caught sight of Hugh farther up the street and waved to him. She had noticed something funny in a shop window and was eager to share the joke with him. Hugh, however, wasn't responding to her smiles and when he came closer, she asked in some concern,

"Hugh, dear, is something wrong?"

Much to her alarm, he didn't even seem to notice her and had a faraway look in his eyes. Then suddenly, he just collapsed into her arms. For one awful moment, Pat thought he had died.

"Can you please help me?" she called out to a man who was nearby, "My husband has heart trouble and something is wrong!"

The passer-by helped her to seat Hugh on the ledge of a shop window and then hurried into the shop to fetch a chair for him. The shopkeeper rang for an ambulance and in no time at all, two kind young ambulance men had arrived. At that moment, Hugh began to come round and announced, as though nothing had happened to him,

"Right, let's get our tea and head for the boat."

He wasn't too pleased when the ambulance men tried to persuade him to get checked out.

"Nonsense," he protested, "I'm fine. Come on, let's go for the boat home."

The ambulance crew won the argument, though Pat began to wonder if she had overreacted, and before long they were following the sign they had joked about earlier – 'To the Hospital'.

Hugh was taken straight to see a doctor and Pat was shown into the waiting room, where she sat in a state of shock. It had all happened so quickly – their plans turned upside down, as they would never make it to the ferry in time for the sailing.

A little later, a nurse called her over and pointed to a room.

"Your husband's in there," she told her.

A doctor was bending over Hugh, attaching wires to him. Hugh gave Pat a frustrated, helpless look which said, 'We could have been heading for the boat and here we are in this place!' Pat began to feel guilty and wondered if she had been wrong to insist on him getting checked out but then she heard the doctor say to Hugh,

"You are having a heart attack!"

All thoughts of catching boats fled as the doctor and nurses worked to reduce his pain and the damage to his heart.

Hugh had to stay in the hospital for a week and Pat found a Bed and Breakfast near the hospital. Richard joined her there and Jonathan looked after James and the house in Carrickfergus. How grateful she was to have sons who cared for her. Friends were also concerned and eager to help. Her friend Anne Cuthbert rang to see if she needed any money. It was obvious that the grocery money was not going to be enough to pay for their stay in the Bed and Breakfast or the food they would need, so Pat told Anne that she intended to use the money they had set aside for bills at home and trust God to supply their need.

Pat was grateful for the kindness of the nurses who attended to Hugh, sorted out the lodgings for her and offered to let her visit the hospital that first night, if she found she couldn't sleep. She was even more grateful for the Lord's provision of a visit from friends. When she woke up in the guest house that first morning, she wondered where she was! As the reality of her situation flooded in, the landlady knocked on her door to tell her that she had visitors. What a comfort it was to find Hugh's cousin, Bobby, his daughter, Christine and her boyfriend there to offer her some support. They had been holidaying in the area too and when Bobby's wife, Eileen, had phoned him to tell him about Hugh, they had gone straight to the hospital, where they had been told the address of the guesthouse. Pat was so glad to see a friendly face.

A week later, Hugh was allowed to travel home and this time they did catch the ferry! The following morning, Pat had a heart-to-heart with God as she stood ironing,

"Lord, You have stood by us throughout these years of Hugh's heart attacks," she told Him. "We ask, dear Lord, for help from on high to meet the payment of the bills – we had to dip in to the money set aside for them while Hugh was in hospital. You have been gracious to bring him home again alive. How I love You."

"Now Lord," she continued, "I'm not much good at counting but I reckon we owe £154. Will You please meet this need?"

Shortly afterwards, there was a knock at the door. It was Reverend Lewis, the minister from Abbotts Cross. Pat switched off the iron and went to chat with him and Hugh in the living room. As he left, he shook Hugh's hand and gave him an envelope.

"The deacons and I have been praying," he explained, "and we felt that you had a need. Would you please accept this gift from the Lord?"

Hugh was speechless and stood looking at the envelope in his hand after the minister left.

"We can't accept this," he said.

When he opened the envelope and told Pat that there was £154 inside, she immediately knew that it was the answer to her prayer that morning. Hugh had known nothing of all the expenses Pat had incurred while he had been lying in hospital but of course God knew and had proved Himself once again to be the great provider. They were even more amazed at God's provision when Hugh returned to his own doctor for a check up.

"You were in the right place at the right time," he told him. "The hospital had just recently been given the latest heart machine, which the doctors used for you. As well as that, the new drug they gave you was extremely expensive, worth about £1200, but it limited the damage to your heart during the heart attack."

God's provision for Pat and Hugh extended beyond Hugh's health. The years had been passing by and Richard had gone off to university, returning home again in his mid twenties. He and Jonathan often met with their friends in the Royal Oak pub in Carrickfergus and sometimes played squash with their friends, Alan and Derek. They had both given up any pretence of interest in Christian things and never really thought about God at all. He had not given up on them of course and one evening, though no one was aware of it, He began to unfold His plan.

Derek was friendly with a young lady called Janet and had a regular session of squash with her. He was unable to fulfil his commitment on this particular evening but had made another arrangement.

"I can't play squash with you next week, Janet," he told her, " but I've asked Richard to play in my place."

Janet was horrified. She had taken a liking to Richard, although she had rarely actually spoken to him, considering him to be way out of her league. She didn't want to be dashing round a squash court with a bright red face, out of breath and exhausted, in front of someone she rather fancied!

"No, honestly, Derek," she protested, "we'll just cancel next week and meet up again in a fortnight's time."

Derek was not to be put off and assured her, "It's no problem, Janet. I've already asked Richard and he said he had no other arrangements and wouldn't mind the extra game."

The next Thursday came and despite Janet's apprehensions, she enjoyed the game. When it was over, to Janet's surprise, Richard asked her for a drink at the Royal Oak. It was the first time they had ever chatted together properly and they found that they really enjoyed one another's company. In the weeks that followed, they met up now and again, discovering that they had a lot in common, including mothers who were both Christians.

Janet was sitting with some friends in the pub one evening when Richard walked in. One of her friends noticed him and said,

"Oh he's gorgeous, he's mine!"

"No no," laughingly protested the other girl, "he's mine!"

Janet found herself thinking, "Well I needn't bother. He wouldn't even look at me."

She had a very good reason for thinking in this way – a little five year old girl, named Claire, who was waiting at home for her. She felt that it would take a special young man to be prepared to accept the responsibility of a ready-made daughter.

Richard, on the other hand, was not put off in the slightest by the idea of a daughter and after a few weeks, asked Janet out. Early on in their relationship, Richard told his mum,

"You know the way you said I would know the right girl? Well I've found her. She has a little girl of five."

"You know," he continued, "when she heard you were Christians, she said you wouldn't have anything to do with me."

His next words thrilled Pat's heart, "I told her that she didn't know my Mum and Dad!"

Pat wasn't entirely surprised to hear what Richard had to say because some weeks earlier, God had begun to prepare her heart. She had been walking round the garden helping Hugh to do some gardening when she had felt God speak to her.

"Hugh," she had announced, "you've to build a hedge and put a gate on it for your grandchildren."

Hugh had looked at her and laughed. "Sure, none of them are even married,"

Despite his laughter, he set to work and not long afterwards, Janet and the little girl who would become their much loved granddaughter, walked in through the gate he had made.

Richard and Janet married in September 1994 and as Pat began to get to know Janet, she recognised in her daughter-in-law a kindred spirit. What she did not realise at that time was that in Janet, God would provide much more than just a daughter-in-law or even a kindred spirit. God had a much bigger plan, for Janet would eventually become a fellow handmaiden.

## Chapter 28
# God's Surprises

AROUND THIS TIME a new sphere of service was opened up for Pat and Hugh, through a visit Pat made to Bobby Logan's mother. They had not seen Bobby or his wife Eileen since they had lived in Greenisland but when Pat heard that his father had died, they decided to visit Auntie May to pass on their sympathy. They were delighted to find the whole family there and to discover that the two daughters, Christine and Heather, had both become Christians. That visit opened up opportunities to work in their schools, Belfast High School and Belfast Royal Academy.

By this time, the prayer meeting that used to be held in Queen Street had been moved to Loughmourne Mission Hall and Christine joined the group of believers who met to call down the blessing of God in that place. She was a lovely singer and Sammy suggested that Pat, Hugh, Christine and himself should practise together so that they could sing in the open airs that had begun again, after Hugh had received a Word from God that guided him in that direction.

"If you will still abide in this land," he read, "then I will build you up and not pull you down. I will plant you and not pluck you up."

The singing group was a great success and resulted in invitations to sing in churches, meeting houses and tent missions. Pat enjoyed this work and they built up good friendships with Christians in many different places – all part of God's plan for their lives.

Meanwhile Pat's brothers and sister had grown up, married and had children of their own. Harold and Pearl had two daughters and a son, Joe and Sally had three sons, Roy and Maureen had two boys and a girl, Noel and Vivienne had two sons, Valerie and Jim had a boy and a girl and they also fostered many children over a period of twenty years. One after the other, Joe, Noel, Roy and Valerie all decided to move to Canada and eventually Pat's parents moved there too.

Joseph died soon after their move and May returned to Carrickfergus. She found it difficult to settle there and went back again to Canada. Soon afterwards, Valerie noticed a black bruise on her mother's leg and, on investigation, a diagnosis of gangrene was made, which resulted in May having to have her leg amputated. She remained in hospital for ten long years, while her health gradually deteriorated. May died in 1995. Harold, who had been very close to his mother, was heartbroken.

At Richard's wedding in September Harold took the opportunity to tell his sister that he too was in poor health but even so, two years later, Pat was shocked when they had a phone call from his daughter, Petula.

"Dad's having a heart attack," she cried down the phone.

Hugh had taken the call and simply told her,

"Hang on – I'll be down."

Pat wasn't going to be left behind and called after him,

"I'm his sister..... take me with you!"

Hugh organised an ambulance and they set off for Harold's house. Harold was lying on the bed when they arrived and Pat was upset to see what she felt was a look of death on his face. Hugh prayed for him that God would spare him. Harold, on the other hand, was more concerned with letting them know how annoyed he was about how it had happened! He had actually taken the attack while out shopping but had somehow managed to get himself home again, only to find the front door locked. He had to struggle round to the back door where his frantic knocking brought someone to the door.

"I'm having a heart attack," he gasped.

The ambulance came soon after they arrived and Harold was admitted to Antrim Hospital. Visiting was limited because he was so ill and Hugh and Pat decided that they would visit only on Sundays. On one of these visits, they were able to speak to the specialist and Hugh asked about Harold's prognosis, explaining that many members of the family lived in Canada and would need as much warning as possible if they were to travel home for his funeral.

The doctor gave Pat a sympathetic look as he said in reply,

"My dear, phone your family now. Your brother will be dead in three days time."

This was a real shock to them as Harold had always looked so well and strong. Their hearts were heavy as they made their way to his bedside. Despite the medication he was on, he was able to chat to them and asked what the weather was like – Pat knew that he was thinking of his garden and how much he enjoyed pottering around in it.

As Hugh began to talk to him, Pat noticed Harold's foot peeping out from under the sheet and she lifted the sheet a little until she could see the scar left by a huge boil that had developed during the war when Harold's health had not been good. She thought of the way he had shouldered the responsibility for the little family at that time and a lump came to her throat as she realised that soon he would be gone.

"Harold," she said very gently, "who knows, you could have another heart attack. Make sure you call on God to save you while you can still think and speak."

Harold's only reply was to ask them to leave so that he could use the bedpan.

As they waited in the corridor outside, Pat and Hugh asked for a Word from God. He gave them Psalm 34 verse 6,

"This poor man cried and the Lord heard him and saved him out of all his troubles."

The nurse was still tidying when they returned and Harold said to them, with a rather smug look on his face,

"There you are Hugh, even the nurse says that no one knows when they are going to die."

He had obviously been quizzing the nurse to see if she knew when he was going to die. Hugh's reply disarmed him,

"That's right, Harold – no man knows – that's why you need to get saved now before it is too late."

He then brought out his Bible and read Psalm 34 to him. About half way through, Pat was afraid that Harold had fallen asleep but when she asked him, she had to laugh at his response,

"Patsy, how can I hear Hugh reading if you keep chirping in?"

They left soon afterwards, content that they had done God's will and content that they could leave the rest in His hands but very aware that they had probably seen Harold for the last time.

Pat spent many days during Harold's illness, wrestling with God on her brother's behalf, greatly distressed that up to this point, Harold had made no public commitment to the Lord.

"This was my brother," she would cry, "who saved my life during the war. I can't let him go to hell!"

As she prayed one day, she sensed that familiar Voice within, assuring her,

"I have heard thy cries."

"Oh God, I hear this voice in my head," she prayed, "but I can't settle for this – it could be from the enemy. I can't afford to be deceived, I need the application of the Spirit to speak and bear witness that it is indeed You speaking!"

Suddenly she felt the Spirit of God rise up within her and all around her, pulling her to her feet and assuring her that God had heard her cries. In the midst of her tears and brokenness, she laughed and danced around the room, so excited that God had answered her prayer. She had no idea that this was just the beginning – that her Heavenly Father was going to give her assurance after assurance, in such miraculous ways, that she would be left with no doubt at all.

Two days before Harold died, Pat and Hugh took advantage of a beautiful day in May to plant out some flowers into the garden. Suddenly she heard God's Voice again,

"I've a wonderful surprise for you on Thursday."

"What is it, Lord," she enquired.

"If I told you, it wouldn't be a surprise!"

Pat wondered if it meant that Harold would die on Thursday but heard no more and contented herself that she could leave it all in the tender care of her God.

In the early hours of Thursday morning, Pat had the first of some rather strange experiences. She had got up to visit the bathroom and as she put her hand on the handle of the toilet, to flush it, she felt as though God opened a lid in her head and she heard a voice that sounded like Harold when he used to pretend to be Churchill – deep and deliberate.

"Listen to the Lord, Patsy," the voice boomed, and then she heard a laugh just like Harold's. "My stubborn will and hardened heart have broken......" Another laugh rang out in the bathroom.

"What a dope I was....... You should see it here, it's so beautiful....... I'm so happy now..........I love you, old girl. Look after the family......and go to Portugal – it's a beautiful country.......I shall see you again."

Pat couldn't believe what she had just heard – she had been praying for Harold in the past years, using those very words – praying that his stubborn will would be broken! As well as that, she had not had the opportunity to tell Harold that she and Hugh were planning to go very soon to Portugal – the very day she had intended to tell him, he had taken the heart attack. She stood there, stunned, unsure how to respond. In the end, she simply looked up, as she would have done to her big brother many times before and like a little girl, said, "Bye-bye, Harold."

She walked unsteadily back into the bedroom and as she sat down on the edge of the bed, the Lord said, "Remember what he said to you."

As a result of this conversation and remembering what the Doctor had said, Pat was fairly sure that Harold was dying and her fears were realised later on in the day. Pat's three brothers and other members of her family were able to fly home for the funeral. Although it was such a sad occasion, there was a certain joy in the reunion and Pat was greatly torn about going to Portugal on holiday. If she cancelled the holiday, she would be able to spend time after the funeral with her family but, on the other hand, she knew that she and Hugh really needed this break and felt that the Lord had provided it for them. The deciding factor in her final decision was the direction she had heard in the bathroom to go to Portugal, so they said their sad farewells to Pat's brothers and set off on their holiday.

On the flight, Pat had a second rather strange experience. At one point on the journey, she looked out the window and to her utter astonishment, saw what looked like an angel flying alongside the plane – holding Harold closely by his side! Pat wasn't sure if she was dreaming or seeing a vision. She wanted to wave to Harold but didn't seem to be able to. Pat put her hand against the window and it seemed as though she heard Harold ask the angel,

"Does she see me?"

"Oh she sees you alright," she heard the angel reply.

At that, Pat turned to Hugh, who was totally oblivious to all of this.

"Harold's out there!" she announced.

It says much for Hugh's calm nature and his understanding of his wife, that the only response he made was, "Is he?"

When Pat looked back again, both Harold and the angel had gone. Was that what God had meant when He had told her of the surprise He had planned for Thursday?

Pat had prayed that the apartment they had booked in Portugal would be clean and bright. It was the last available room at the top of the building and she was so afraid it would be dingy or brown. She needn't have worried for, after struggling up four flights of stairs with their luggage, they opened the door of the apartment, to find white floors and walls, even a white breakfast bar – very clean and very bright!

They were tired after travelling and after the stress of the previous weeks so it wasn't long before they were in bed. But God wasn't finished with His surprise just yet – Hugh fell asleep first and as Pat lay in the darkness, she saw the angel and Harold standing at the bottom of the bed. She lay completely still as the angel told her,

"Pat, Harold and I are leaving now. When you wake up tomorrow morning, that will begin your holiday. Enjoy it."

Pat did just that – she and Hugh relaxed and enjoyed their time in the sun. Not surprisingly, she thought often about those strange experiences. She was, of course, comforted by them as they confirmed to her that her much-loved brother was in Heaven and each time she thought of him in the company of angels, joy rose up in place of the grief she felt. She did feel, however, that they were the sort of experiences that could not be shared with everyone and for many years afterwards, she kept them secret and, like Mary of old, pondered them in her heart.

## Chapter 29
# Voice of Warning

PAT WOKE IN the early hours of a September morning later that year. God was calling her to pray so she got up in obedience to His call. She made her way to the living room and began to sing praises to her God. Although she had no idea why He had called her to pray, she knew that as she came in obedience to His Throne of grace, He would give her the insight she needed. There was a powerful sense of His Presence in the room and soon she knew that she should move over to the conservatory doors. For some time now, holding on to the door handles in the conservatory had been her trysting place with God. As she prepared her heart for battle and waited on His Word, He showed her that the enemy was planning to stop the open-air meetings. Bit by bit, He revealed the plan to her: the shopkeepers, led by a newcomer who had taken over a café, were plotting to stop the open-air in the Market Place. They had gone to the Council and that very day, a councillor would confront the group with the intention of removing them.

Pat stood at the doors and made intercession against the plans of the enemy. She cried out to God until she knew the battle was over and then asked God for confirmation from His Word. She read Psalm 28 verses 4 and 5, which spoke about the opposition she had sensed:

"Give them according to their deeds and according to the wickedness of their endeavours: give them after the work of their hands: render to them their desert. Because they regard not the works of the Lord, nor the operation of His hands, He shall destroy them and not build them up."

Then she was led to Isaiah chapter 54 verse 15, God's promise to her heart that His hand was on the whole situation:

"Behold they shall surely gather together but not by me: whosoever shall gather together against thee shall fall for thy sake."

Pat thanked and praised God for His wonderful love and the mercy He showed to His own. There was no need for Him to give a warning of the enemy's intentions but by His grace, had allowed her to have a part in His plan of vindication.

She returned to bed and slept for the few hours that were left of the night. When she woke, she wasn't sure if her experience had been real or a dream but she felt in her heart that she had not been dreaming. She told Hugh about it and later shared her experience with the group as they gathered for the open-air. They prayed together, committing themselves and the outcome of the day to Jesus, and the meeting started. The music from the café blared out at full volume as the shoppers made their way along the street. They noticed some of the shop assistants looking out now and again, obviously anticipating with some relish the moment when the council would arrive and rid them of the nuisance of these open-air fanatics. A sports car raced by and the two young men in it shouted insults at the group, waving their arms in triumph as they sped past.

"We've got you now!" they seemed to be saying.

Just then a policeman and policewomen walked slowly by but Pat and her friends just continued with the meeting and they made no approach to them. Half way through the meeting, a girl from the Council arrived. She strolled over towards Pat and asked her,

"Who's in charge?"

"Mr Logan, the man at the microphone," Pat replied. "He'll be finished shortly."

When Hugh had finished preaching, Pat introduced him to the Councillor who told him,

"People have been complaining about your meeting."

"Is that right?" Hugh responded, "Can I enquire who is doing the complaining?"

"I'm not permitted to say," the councillor told him.

"How long have these meetings been going on?" she enquired.

She looked really surprised when Hugh said,

"Fourteen years, without a complaint, except for one woman – the previous owner of the café asked us if we could move a little further down the street and we did so as we didn't want to cause offence."

Meanwhile the meeting had continued and the singing began.

"Is this the volume the music is kept at?" she asked.

Hugh assured her that it was. On hearing that, she smiled, shook hands with Hugh and told him,

"I have no complaint with it. I wish you the very best."

As she walked away the café owner turned the volume of his music up as loudly as possible, as though in protest but there was nothing he could do – God had decided the outcome. Pat and Hugh were amazed to learn that within a week, the café had to close down but their faithful work for God in that place continued for many years.

## Chapter 30
# Foretaste of Revival

FROM TIME TO time, Pat would feel greatly burdened for her boys and would spend many hours weeping for them and wrestling in prayer for them. It hurt her deeply to see them expend all their energies on the things of the world with little thought of God. One night she was feeling the burden of it all particularly keenly and just cried out to God in despair,

"God, enough is enough – surely it is time for these lads to be saved!"

At that moment a vision flashed across her mind – the eldest boy, Richard was running along beside her, taking the banner of the Lord out of her hand, saying as he did so,

"Mother, take hold of my hand. I am here to fight the battle."

She held on to the promise of that vision, though she did not see its fulfilment for some time. Meanwhile, she was grateful to God when Richard married Janet and even more so when she saw how well they all got on during the months they spent living together in 1997 as they waited for Richard and Janet's house to be built.

When Jonathan met a young lady called Maureen in the April of that year, she watched with interest as their relationship grew. Would this be the Lord's choice for him?

At first it didn't seem that the relationship would last. They were two very different people, had different friends, were of a different age group and had little in common except a restlessness of spirit that nothing seemed to satisfy. Their friends disapproved of their relationship and even Maureen's family were unsure of what was best for her.

Jonathan invited Maureen to go to Donegal for a weekend with some of his friends but by the end of the first day, they had quarrelled and agreed to part company on their return home. Then in the evening they went for a walk along the beautiful beach and sat for a while on the sand. Their conversation turned to God and to their surprise they both felt that in some strange way, He was communicating with them, assuring them that He was real and that He was there, present with them. The following day they knew that something had shifted in their relationship – God's love had been made manifest in their hearts.

Despite this experience, their friendship still seemed held together by a slender thread. In the months that followed, Jonathan's discontent became greater and as Maureen watched the roller coaster of his emotions, she found herself crying out to God on his behalf. There were times when he seemed to want to have nothing to do with God and then there were other times when he would go to his parents and ask them to pray for a Word from God for him. When Pat and Hugh would give him God's Word, Maureen would take comfort in the verses, clinging to them as she watched Jonathan's agony of spirit. She was so concerned for him that she didn't realise that God's Voice was calling out to her as well.

Things became so bad between them that by January of the next year, they decided to take a break from one another. Maureen thought that the heartache she was experiencing would stop when she stopped seeing Jonathan but soon discovered otherwise! The night after they broke up, she visited Pat and Hugh to return something she had borrowed. Of course the conversation soon turned to God, as was customary in their home. Both Pat and Hugh talked at some length to Maureen and she shared with them that she knew she needed to get right with God.

"Would you like to come to Jesus now?" they asked but Maureen was a shy girl and declined. In her heart, however, she determined to seek the Lord when she returned to her own home.

When she reached her house, she opened her door, climbed the stairs, threw herself down on the bed and cried out to God for salvation. Immediately light filled her heart and she saw Jesus dying on the cross for her sin. Her heart was broken in that instant and she found forgiveness and peace with God through the sacrifice of Jesus at Calvary. She rose from her knees a new person, complete in Him. It was 28th January and though she didn't know it at the time, this date would mark what would be the beginning of a mini-Revival in Pat's family.

Maureen didn't realise that she should speak to others about her conversion so when she went shopping with Pat the following evening, she said nothing. They talked about the Lord while shopping and on returning home, read the Bible and prayed together. Pat was puzzled by this stage.

"How can I be having such sweet fellowship with this young girl," she wondered, "when she isn't even saved yet, as far as I know?"

She shared with Maureen what was on her heart and Maureen told her what had taken place the previous night. How Pat's heart rejoiced!

Jonathan made contact with Maureen that Saturday, saying that he wanted to meet up. Maureen took the opportunity during that meeting to tell him what had happened to her and to invite him to go with her to a Mission being held in Moy. She had agreed to go with Pat and Hugh. The speaker was a young man called Alan Bartley whom Pat and Hugh knew through the Lisburn Lifeboat Mission. They had begun to attend the meetings in Lisburn, drawn to them because of the desire the evangelists shared to see Revival come to Ireland. Alan Bartley was the main evangelist but others, including Gilbert Egerton and Dwain Russell, also preached in the Mission from time to time. They had previously invited Richard and Jonathan and their girlfriends to one of the Saturday night rallies but on that occasion, the two boys couldn't wait to get out of the meeting and had headed straight to the pub!

The response on that Sunday night, 1st February, in Moy, however, was somewhat different. Alan Bartley spoke on the Prodigal Son and Jonathan felt as though God was speaking directly to him. He waited afterwards to talk to Alan and prayed the sinner's prayer before he left. He didn't have any real sense of assurance and so, as he shook Alan's hand, he thought to himself,

"You won't be seeing me again!"

How wrong he was. Over the next few days, he became more and more convinced of his salvation, until he was completely certain that he belonged to Jesus and that Jesus belonged to him. He and Maureen began to spend time with Pat and Hugh, talking about the Lord and singing His praise together.

A few weeks later, Richard rang Jonathan during one of these times of fellowship to ask him if he would like to join him for a walk in the Mournes on the following day, a Sunday. To Richard's surprise, Jonathan's reply was,

"I'm not sure, I'll go and pray about it."

Was this the same brother, Richard wondered, who was usually more concerned about where to go for a pint?

Jonathan shared what Richard had said with Maureen and his Mum and Dad. They prayed together and then Jonathan and Maureen went home. Jonathan felt that he should go with Richard but asked God to confirm that decision – if it was truly of God, the sun would be shining the next day and the skies would be blue.

Meanwhile Richard had his own revelation from God that night! In his dream, he could see Jonathan and himself climbing the Mourne Mountains. The sun was shining and the sky was blue. When they arrived at the top of one of the mountains, Richard got saved. Richard shared this with Janet and asked her,

"If I went up the Mournes with Jonathan and came home saved, what would you think?"

"I wouldn't be surprised," Janet replied.

Next morning, the sun was shining and the sky was blue so the two young men headed off at eight o'clock in the morning. Jonathan had promised that he wouldn't preach at Richard but his heart was so full of joy that he couldn't help talking about Jesus. Unknown to him, of course, God had already been working in Richard's heart. As they came to the first mountain peak, Richard found himself saying over and over to himself,

"Ask me, Jonathan, if I want to get saved."

Jonathan didn't ask him anything - just kept talking as they threw down their rucksacks and stopped for something to eat, admiring the wonderful view as they ate. When they once again lifted their rucksacks to set out for the next peak, Richard thought,

"Well, maybe at the next mountain, I'll get saved."

Then another thought flashed across his mind,

"I may never reach the next mountain!"

He threw down his rucksack and said,

"Jonathan, I want to give my life to the Lord. Will you pray for me?"

Jonathan was rather taken aback and panicked for a moment,

"What do I know about prayer?" he said. He soon recovered and the two brothers knelt on the mountain top so that Richard could commit his life to the Lord. It was 22nd February, just three weeks after Jonathan's conversion. The rest of their walk was spent singing God's praise and talking about the Lord.

The following Saturday, 28th February, Richard and Janet joined Pat and Hugh for lunch and had agreed to go to a rally in the Lisburn Lifeboat Mission that evening. It had not been a good week for them – Richard had been ill with 'flu' and had spent most of the week lying on their settee in front of the fire. Janet had also spent a miserable week but for an entirely different reason – God had been working in her heart, making her aware of her sin. She struggled through the lunch, finding the company of the others almost unbearable. She just had to get away so she made an excuse about doing shopping and left the house. As she walked past the shoppers, she felt that she must surely be the most miserable person of them all.

Although Richard still felt unwell, he really believed that it was important to go to the meeting so he and Janet set out for Lisburn. He had no idea just how important it would prove to be!

Alan Bartley was the speaker and his wife, Rachel, gave her testimony. There was a real sense of the Presence of God in the meeting. They spent some time in silence at the end, waiting on God. Anne Davidson and her husband, Robert, had gone with them and she looked rather ill at ease during this time – she felt that God was telling her to speak to Janet but could see no way of doing so. Richard wasn't feeling too well and he decided that he and Janet shouldn't stay for supper but should go on home. Pat was aware of what was happening and sensed that the enemy would use this to get Janet out of the way – she knew by looking at Janet's face that she was under conviction of sin. So she told Richard to pray about his decision and turned back round to pray herself. A moment later, she realised that Janet had left the room.

Meanwhile, Janet's misery had become worse and worse as the meeting progressed. Her whole being felt heavy so when Richard talked about going home, part of her felt glad.

"Here's your chance to leave," she thought to herself.

"No," another voice inside her argued, "I've got to get this sorted out with God now!"

She left her seat to look for Alan but couldn't find him so she took refuge in the toilet and began to cry, breaking her heart, asking God to send someone to her. At that moment there was a knock on the door and a soft voice said,

"Janet, it's me, Anne. Open the door and let me in."

Janet brushed the tears from her eyes and opened the door. As they hugged each other, they both knew that this was Janet's time to be born anew. They knelt down and Anne had the joy of pointing this lovely young lady to the Lord – a special joy for her as most of those she led to the Lord were the dying men and women she nursed.

When Pat looked back on that amazing month, in which Richard and Janet, Jonathan and Maureen all became followers of Jesus, she felt she had indeed been given a foretaste of Revival. She had made no special effort for their salvation at that time – God had simply swept them one by one into His Kingdom. What a joy it was to realise that they too had heard the Voice in the laburnum tree and that they now could stand beside her in the battle, carrying the banner she had seen in her vision. It was a wonderful experience, the culmination of years of prayers and tears on their behalf. Psalm 126 verse 2 summed up how Pat and Hugh felt when God accomplished such a miracle in their family:

"Our mouths were filled with laughter, our tongues with songs of joy. Then it was said among the nations – the Lord has done great things for them."

If God could do such a miracle in her family, He could certainly do a similar miracle for His handmaiden in her land. How she longed to see Revival come to Carrickfergus, to her beloved Ireland. As the singing ministry they had been involved in seemed to close, this call to deep intercessory prayer grew ever stronger. As soon as the younger members of the family became Christians, they joined Pat and Hugh in this ministry and God began to place in their hearts the same burden for their homeland. During this period, Maureen was called to spend six months in the Faith Mission, where God touched her heart with the cry for Revival and gave her a deep insight into the ministry of prayer.

For six years they met to pray for Revival. Eventually they felt called to spend Sunday mornings in prayer instead of attending a church service. They were obedient to His call, despite the realisation that many would not understand why they were doing this. By that stage, Richard and Janet's new house had been completed so they decided that the six of them would meet for this time of prayer in the new house. And God chose to bless this little group who met in obedience to Him, who had felt His heartbeat for their town and their country and He graced them with His divine Presence. His Voice spoke often to their hearts and minds, passing on His Word for lost and hurting people and for their torn and broken province.

## Chapter 31
# Holidays or Holy Days?

HOLIDAYS FOR PAT and Hugh had been spent in Ireland when the boys were small and then later on in England, Scotland or Wales. They brought a tent and enjoyed many wonderful holidays exploring the beauties of the mainland. They hadn't been abroad since their holiday to Portugal until the year in which Jonathan and Maureen got married, 2001. In January of that year, Pat had wakened from sleep with the words, "Go to Austria, it's now or never!" ringing in her ears. Despite the fact that they had no money to go, Pat sensed that this was of God and shared it with the family.

Jonathan and Maureen's wedding was planned for June and they offered to go with Pat and Hugh in September. Jonathan was very enthusiastic about it all.

"This could be a one off," he said excitedly, "I feel we should hire a car and tour a couple of other places."

They all agreed with his suggestion and Jonathan made the arrangements for their journey. Pat didn't realise as they set off for Brussels and then Germany, that while they had planned holidays, God had planned holy days!

From Germany, they headed off for a tour of Austria and Italy, stopping for a few days in various places along the way. Pat felt as though God Himself travelled with them, a divine tour guide of His amazing creation.

"Pat, you're going to love this place," she would hear Him say, as they travelled to Venice, Tuscany and Lake Garda. Each fresh beauty took her breath away and her heart sang out in praise and adoration to a God whose companionship added such pleasure to each day's discoveries.

They stayed at Zell-am-see and it was here that God revealed to Pat that He had a deeper purpose for her holiday. They took a cable car to the top of one of the snow-covered mountains – how excited Pat was as the little car swung out from its station and seemed to dangle in space. She gazed at the vista that stretched out on all sides as the car slowly carried them to the peak – green meadows, giving way to tree-covered slopes and finally, the snowline! They stepped from the cable car, breathing in the pure, crisp air at the summit and decided to take some time just to be on their own. Pat chose a spot where she could be alone and stood, awestruck by the beautiful scene before her. All around her were snow-covered peaks and she started to laugh – it looked like a giant pavlova! As she drank it all in, the still air carried the tinkle of the cowbells up from the lower slopes of the valley – what delicate music, the sort of sound she imagined she might hear in Heaven.

All of a sudden, she knew a strong sense of the Presence of God. She was on her own with Him and He poured out on her once again the deep ministry of intercession that He had given to her many times before. She began to weep as God impressed upon her the enormous need of the people of Austria and the great depth of His love for them. She felt something of His heart for the people in this beautiful land and her own heart broke as she cried aloud and made intercession for them. Her body ached with a passionate yearning for their salvation – no longer just another tourist in the mighty Alps, but a handmaiden of the Lord, fulfilling His purposes for her life.

When the intercession ceased, she wiped away her tears and began to worship, her song of praise and adoration ringing out in the stillness. She knew He had heard her cry, she knew He would answer her prayer and her heart leapt with joy. As she made her way to join the rest of the family, she rejoiced in a God who could turn a holiday into a holy day.

God ministered to her in a different way on one of the evenings when they were staying in a typically Austrian hotel in the Tyrol. The hotel was situated in the centre of the valley, with high green mountains on both sides and a magnificent snow-covered mountain in the distance. Summer and winter seemed to exist at the same time in that magical place. Pat had been up in the early hours of the morning and was about to get back in to bed when she heard the Voice speaking to her.

"Go to the balcony doors and look out," He instructed.

It was almost dawn and soon the darkness would give way to the light of a new day. For some reason, Pat felt excited and full of wonder – what was happening, what did God have to show her?

She opened the doors and stepped out on to the balcony. She could smell the scent of the flowers wafting in the night air. Down in the valley tiny lights appeared as little villages here and there began to awaken. As she looked to her left, she caught sight of a small, round, red brick chimney pot, a little trail of white smoke curling from it. Pat caught her breath as she realised why God had told her to go outside – He was going to restore to her something of the childhood she had lost as she grew up in a war-torn London. The sense of responsibility she had felt, having to care for the younger members of her family and often for a sick mother too, had smothered any childish sense of excitement at Christmas and the coming of a present-bearing Santa. What she saw before her was like a scene from a Christmas card, a real, living Christmas scene. All at once she became a child again, a child full of excitement and she called out into the night,

"Santa's coming!"

"God really does restore to us the years the locusts have eaten," she thought as she made her way back to bed, enveloped in a lovely sense of peace and well-being. What a wonderful love-token from her Heavenly Father.

Pat had another call to intercession some years later while on holiday in France, this time with Richard and Janet and the granddaughters, Claire, Rebekah and Amy. They were staying in a caravan park in Brittany and Pat had been hurrying to finish reading a book that she wanted to loan to Janet. She felt her heart stir as she finished the book but picked it up and left the caravan to find Janet. Then suddenly she once again sensed the call to deep intercession. Her immediate response was one of panic

– should she return to the caravan? How deep would this intercession be? Would her loud cries disturb others in the caravans nearby?

She had just decided to walk close to her own caravan when the intercession began and her tears began to flow. This time she pleaded on behalf of the people of France, crying aloud to God for the salvation of the people of this new country she was visiting. The burden was deep and heavy but eventually her tears lessened and she sensed in her spirit that God had something else on His heart. What could it be? As she looked up through eyes that were blurred with tears, she saw some young people walking in the distance along a path to her left. She only realised that Claire was one of their number when she waved at Pat. As she lifted her hand to return the greeting, the Spirit prompted her to pray for her lovely granddaughter.

The following week was spent at another campsite which Pat really loved. The family spent a lot of time at the pool, enjoying the warmth of the sun and the coolness of the pool. One morning Janet left to do some washing in the laundrette and Pat told her she wouldn't be joining the family at the pool that day as she felt called to stay in the caravan and pray. She lifted some of the cushions off the settee to kneel on while she waited for His Word to her heart.

"Lay another cushion out on the floor for Janet," His Voice told her, "she'll be joining you."

Just then the caravan door opened and in walked Janet.

"God spoke to me in the laundrette and told me to join you," she said.

Their fellowship that morning was sweet as the Holy Spirit led them to intercede together. The hours flew by – another holiday had been transformed into a holy day! Moments like these reminded Pat of the verse in Psalm 2:

"Ask of Me and I shall give thee the heathen for thine inheritance and the uttermost parts of the earth for thy possession."

The Christmas holidays of 2003 also included a wonderful holy day. In the early hours of Boxing Day, she was awakened by the Lord speaking to her.

"Pat," He reminded her, "you didn't receive a Christmas card from June, with one of her newsy letters."

She got up straight away and checked all the cards that were on display in the living room.

"Lord, You're right," she said, "Something must be wrong. That's not like June."

She remembered then, how, early in December when the cards first started to arrive, that she had looked out for a card from June but then the days got busy closer to Christmas day and it all went out of her mind again.

"Lord, You're so good to remind me," she told Him, "I'll give her a wee ring later on after the prayer meeting."

June had been their friend for many years and had proved to be one of those special 'friends in need' at a time when Pat and Hugh really needed help. She had invited them to share her home when they had nowhere to live and Pat and Hugh had never forgotten her for that. They had kept in touch every year at Christmas since that time and Pat often thought of her and prayed for her as she knew that June had not yet become a Christian. Pat shared her concern with the family when they met to pray that Sunday morning and Jonathan too felt worried.

"Mum, ring June," he said. "It's not like her, she always sends you a card and a letter at Christmas. Something must be wrong."

"Yes, you're right," Pat responded, "I'll ring her after lunch."

When the family had gone, Pat rang June, who was now living in York. When the call went through, Pat spoke first,

"Hello June – it's Pat. How are you?"

She was shocked when a soft frail voice replied,

"Oh Pat, I'm ill."

"What's wrong, dear?" Pat asked.

"I have cancer of the lung, the worst sort," came the reply.

Pat hesitated about asking her next question but felt she needed to know.

"Is it to the death?"

"Yes," June whispered softly. This conversation was like no other they had ever shared before – usually they giggled and laughed together as they got caught up on each other's news.

"Would you say you need a miracle?" Pat asked.

"Yes, I would," June replied.

"Okay, June, I'm going to pray with you for a miracle," Pat announced and proceeded to pray with her over the telephone. When she put the phone down, Pat thought about her friend – the only unsaved friend who had kept in touch with her during the previous forty-four years. Despite being shocked by the sad news, Pat didn't feel downcast for somehow she sensed that God was in control of the whole situation. She was puzzled because usually when they spoke on the phone, Pat would talk to June about God but this time, when she was in greater need than ever before, Pat had felt no liberty to speak of her salvation. She was still wondering about this when she went to bed.

The Lord woke her out of a deep sleep.

"Pat, get up and intercede for June," He urged.

As she entered the living room, the Holy Spirit spoke into her heart,

"Pat, you couldn't understand why you didn't have the liberty to point June to the Lord for salvation when you were praying for her healing and this is why. The enemy is using two agents against her and I want you to come against them in the Name of Jesus and break their power over her so that she can be delivered from them and come to Him for salvation."

Pat prayed earnestly against the power of the enemy until she sensed that the battle had been won.

The following day, she had an appointment with the doctor to get a steroid injection for pain in her shoulder. It was a cold day and she wasn't feeling very well so when she arrived home, she was delighted to see that Hugh had lit the fire – how comforting it was to see the flames blazing in the hearth and feel their warmth. She had just settled into her seat when the phone rang and Hugh went to answer it.

"Oh hello, June," she could hear him saying, "yes, she's here. I'll pass you on to her."

He handed Pat the phone and as they began to chat, she shared what had happened to her in the night. Suddenly she sensed the freedom she had missed the previous afternoon and began to talk to June about salvation.

"You know, June," she told her, "I would carry you on my back if I could for salvation but, Love, it's between you and God."

They talked on and then June suddenly said,

"Pat, I want to get saved."

"Really, June?"

"Yes," she replied and Pat had the great joy of leading her friend to the Lord. What a wonderful moment – another holy day.

It didn't end there because God did a further miracle – a miracle of healing. The tumour began to shrink, astounding the doctors and nurses who were treating her. Each time Pat and she talked on the phone, her voice sounded stronger. What a thrill it was for Pat to hear June talk about her Saviour. Soon she was strong enough to travel to Ireland on a short visit to her sister.

Out of the blue, one day during their visit, her husband Bill surprised her by saying,

"June, you probably wouldn't agree with me but I would love to sell up in York and come to live here."

June was delighted and immediately responded,

"Oh Bill, I would love that,"

Her treatment was almost finished so they put their house up for sale. Their next-door neighbour asked to view it and offered to buy it right away! June began to realise that God was in control and she was utterly convinced of it when they started looking at property in Ireland. They went to view a four-bedroom house but the owners weren't in. As they stood looking at the outside of the house, they heard someone ask,

"Can I help you?"

It was the next-door neighbour, calling to them from his garden. When they explained that they had come to see the house he asked,

"Would you like to view ours? It has only three bedrooms."

This actually suited them better and so they went in to his house, liked what they saw and offered to buy it! The sale went through smoothly and it wasn't long before they were settled into their new home.

For eighteen months, June had good health against all medical expectations but then the cancer returned and on that occasion, it claimed her life. In those months, her changed life and deep love for Jesus, as well as her peace when death finally came, was a wonderful witness to her family and friends. How thankful Pat was that once more she had obeyed the Voice she had first heard in the laburnum tree all those years ago and had risen from her bed to pray for an old friend.

Chapter 32
# His Voice Still Speaks

ONE BY ONE the cars arrived at Jonathan and Maureen's home. It was a dry, bright Sunday morning in August 2007, a welcome change to the dull, wet days of the rest of that summer. Hugh carried his accordion into the front room, Pat, Janet, Maureen, Richard and Jonathan took their seats and the children left their toys to join the adults. Amy and Rebekah curled up beside Richard and Janet, Isaiah climbed unto Jonathan's knee and little Seth just managed to fit on Maureen's lap, somewhat hampered by the bump that in a few weeks' time would become a little brother for the two boys.

"Now," said Hugh, as he lifted up the accordion, "who's going to give out the hymnbooks?"

Isaiah ran to the table where the books were sitting and passed them around the family. Before they began to sing, Janet read some verses that spoke of how God clothes His people in garments of salvation and robes of righteousness.

"You know," she remarked, "we used to wear garments of sin but God has forgiven us and taken them away and given us new garments of salvation."

The others nodded their assent to what she had said and then the time of worship began. The little ones tried to join in with the grown up hymns as best they could and when it came to the children's choruses that each child was encouraged to choose, the adults did the actions too, even when it involved marching round the lounge, singing 'I'm in the Lord's army'!

The children's songs gave way to some of the great old hymns of praise and adoration. The group was small but they sang with sincerity and the words of 'Praise My Soul the King of Heaven' and 'O Worship the King' were offered up out of hearts that were full of appreciation to God. The deep longings and desires of those hearts were expressed in the lines of Oliver Holmes' hymn, 'Lord of All Being, Throned Afar',

"Lord of all life, below, above,
Whose light is truth, whose warmth is love,
Before Thy ever-blazing throne,
We ask no lustre of our own.

Grant us Thy truth, to make us free,
And kindling hearts that burn for Thee,
Till all Thy living altars claim
One holy light, one heavenly flame."

The sense of the Presence of God was very real as the words of one of Faber's hymns rang out in that room and ascended up to Heaven itself, a sweet-smelling sacrifice of praise to the Almighty,

"How wonderful, how beautiful
The sight of Thee must be,
Thine endless wisdom, boundless power,
And awful purity."

A hush descended on the little group as the reality of the greatness and power of God was once more impressed on their minds. How amazing to think that despite His Glory and Holiness, He would choose to meet with them, six ordinary men and women in a home in Carrickfergus. Pat and Hugh and their two sons with their wives and children had been meeting together for some time, ever since they all had sensed a call from God deep within their spirits, to stop attending the morning service each Sunday and instead spend that time in prayer. The two hours they spent in Jonathan's home each week had proved to be a great blessing to all of them, as they encouraged each other in the Lord and gave themselves to the vital role of prayer warriors for the nation.

When the worship time finished, the little ones went to the family room for their stories and activities, while the adults settled to listen for God's Word to their hearts and His prompting for their prayers. Jonathan read Psalm 1 and also some of the Beatitudes and recalled how his meditation on these passages through the previous week had caused a great upsurge of thanksgiving in his heart, as he realised just how much God had blessed him and his family.

Before the little group started to pray, Richard shared some verses that had struck him very forcefully during the week, linking them with the excitement he had felt when he had heard about a group of Christians who had been meeting to study God's Word in County Clare.

"We need to be praying for groups like this," he urged the others. "The enemy would just love to cut them down before they manage to grow strong in the Lord."

The mention of believers in the South of Ireland reminded Pat of the group she had visited in County Cork.

"Groups like these need to be linked together," she said, "and that would help to strengthen them."

With that, the Logan family set themselves to prayer, some turning to kneel in front of their chairs and others just remaining seated. Soon, the air was filled with earnest pleas and loud cries as they stormed the very gates of Heaven on behalf of brothers and sisters all over Ireland, many of whom they had never even met but for whom God had given them a passion. As Hugh drew his prayer to a close, he remembered the years he had spent playing his trumpet in the band and he compared the pleasure he had known then to his present experience,

"What greater joy could there be," he cried out to God, "than to be on my knees, pleading for the souls of men!"

One after another they took up the baton of prayer, beseeching their Father in Heaven to pour out His Spirit on the land of Ireland, to break the chains of unbelief that hold so many in bondage, to shine the light of His love on the hearts of men and women, to bring Revival once more to the land of 'saints and scholars'. And as they waited in His Presence, they sensed Him draw near, confirming to them His call upon their lives. It was a high calling, to holiness and obedience and a life of service.

Pat sat on the settee and knew a deep sense of contentment. She had been listening to the Voice of God for many years, a voice first heard from the vibrant yellow blossom of a laburnum tree. She had devoted her life to obeying His Voice and had seen His mighty hand at work in her life. Now, in these prayer times, she was beginning to see the fulfilment of the dream she had had of Richard asking her to pass on the banner to him. He had indeed taken up the banner and God had given him a similar passion to her own for the people of Ireland. She had listened to Jonathan bring a Word from God to the group and in her heart she whispered,

"His Voice still speaks!"

She thought of her two daughters-in-law, the next generation of handmaidens, young women whose tongues had been touched by coals of fire from Heaven. She said 'Amen' to Maureen's prayers of longing for an increased intimacy with God and an increased usefulness in His service. Her spirit rose up in strong agreement as she listened to Janet's prayer.

"What greater work could we be involved in?" Janet asked as she cried out to God for His blessing and the outpouring of His power.

There was, of course, still an ache in her heart – an overwhelming longing to see her third son and his wife share their passion – but she had trusted God for Richard and Jonathan and she knew she could trust Him for James too. There was also a great unfulfilled desire that was never far from her thoughts – a passionate desire for Revival. She had caught tiny glimpses of what it might look like and those glimpses had just strengthened her longing to see Revival blessing in her day. God had called His handmaiden to listen for His Voice, to obey it without question and to pray for Revival – she would do so for the rest of the days He would grant to her. Oh that others across the world might catch the vision and join her in calling down the fire of Heaven in a mighty outpouring that would see the men and women of Ireland cry out in repentance, that would see the transformation of a land and its people and that would see the angels of Heaven rejoicing over lost souls being swept into the Kingdom of God!

# Epilogue
# Building Inspection

THE TWO ANGELS set out across Heaven for the Annual Building Inspection. The young apprentice was excited – it was his first inspection.

"How wonderful it will be to see the amazing mansions being prepared for the King's chosen ones!" he called out to the senior angel as they flew along, faster then any movement earth has ever known.

"Well, here's our first stop," the reply boomed across, "let's see what you think of these."

The sign at the entrance to the building site said 'Evangelist Everglade' and the apprentice stopped for a moment to take in the busy scene. The angelic builders were hard at work erecting structures of all shapes and sizes on the solid foundations that had been laid all over the site. Large rumbling trucks delivered piles of shining bricks here and there and as they tumbled out in front of the structures, the angels set to work.

The apprentice recognized the name on one of the mansions and was rather surprised that the house was so small.

"I thought this would be a huge mansion by now – he is so well known on earth and preaches to great crowds of people all the time."

The wise old angel smiled,

"Yes, that's right but take a look at what happens to the bricks he keeps sending up to us."

The apprentice took a closer look – as the builders tried to set the bricks in place, they crumbled in their hands.

"What's the problem?" he enquired.

"Well, you see, the bricks he sends are made of pride and self-sufficiency and they're just no use for buildings in Heaven."

The next house wasn't much bigger and again the young angel questioned why.

"I've watched him preach – he's so passionate, so clever with words. People flock to hear him and watch him on television too. Is there something wrong with his bricks too?"

His mentor nodded and indicated that he should watch the builders. He was amazed to see that although the bricks appeared to be strong and solid, they cracked and split as the builders tried to put them into place and one after another had to be discarded.

"The cracks are caused by errors. This evangelist doesn't always preach the Truth. Instead he speaks words that the people like to hear. The King has decreed that unless bricks are based on Truth, they can't be used."

The young apprentice moved on to another part of the site where a substantial, two-storey mansion was nearing completion.

"Now, this one has an interesting story," said the senior angel. "This man has never preached from a pulpit in his life and, outside his own community, no one has ever heard of him."

"So how did he manage to have a mansion like this built for him?" asked his companion.

"Well, the King gave him the same gift as the others, the gift of evangelism and he uses it almost every day. He tells everyone he meets about the Master and His salvation and every week the trucks deliver a supply of faithfulness bricks. They're great bricks for building – no crumbling or cracks at all."

The two inspectors left Evangelist Everglade and flew on, stopping now and then to carry out inspections on Missionary Meadows, Pastors Park, Elders Estate and Sunday School Teachers Terrace. The apprentice was excited to see all the building work and marvelled at the diversity of bricks being delivered and the magnificent mansions being designed and created from them. He was particularly impressed by a large mansion in Missionary Meadows, of intricate design and built to the highest specification. He was sure it must belong to the head of some great missionary organisation but was astonished to find that its owner was an elderly woman who had spent her life in a remote area with a little-known tribe, learning their difficult language and sharing their hardships.

"Her mansion is made of some of the finest bricks – bricks of sacrifice and service," the senior angel explained. "Up here we don't have the same values as they do down there."

They flew on and the young angel's excitement began to change to dismay as a huge expanse of what looked like one of earth's shanty towns came into sight. He noticed that good, strong foundations were in place everywhere in this great area but the structures were small and unstable, rickety houses made from bits of wood and even straw. Many of the angelic builders sat in the middle of bare foundations, glum looks on their faces. A lone truck drove through the vast site, offloading a few bricks here and there.

"What is going on here?" the trainee inspector asked in astonishment.

"I hate having to inspect this area – we call it the Just Saved Site. So little building gets done here because the people send up so few bricks or send inferior materials. They seem to think that just being saved is the end of it all but of course we know it is actually the beginning."

"But hasn't anyone told them about working out their salvation?" the young angel enquired.

"Oh yes," came the reply, "many people have tried. The Master Himself spoke of it often when He visited earth. He told stories about using talents and seeking the lost, He taught about prayer and forgiveness, He modelled love and compassion in His own life but they don't seem to grasp it at all."

"What a shame," the young angel sighed, "this could be such a wonderful place."

"Oh let's move on," said his companion, "the last site on our list should cheer you up."

They flew past a sign that read 'Handmaiden Heights', gave a nod of satisfaction as they circled a group of modest but very attractive mansions and stopped in front of two rather beautiful houses, gleaming in the Light of Heaven.

"Now that's what I would call mansions," breathed the young angel as he gazed at the brilliant facades. "But I don't understand," he went on, as he checked the nameplates, "the owners are just handmaidens – they haven't done anything spectacular, nobody knows about them, their stories weren't told in the newspapers, they never went overseas......"

His protests died away as the other angel looked at him.

"It's all to do with Kingdom values," he reminded his young assistant. He pointed to the first mansion.

"This one is being built almost entirely of obedience bricks – that's why the whole house shines like gold. The King's servants hear the His Voice, sometimes in the oddest of places, in bedrooms or bathrooms, even in laburnum trees! They obey instantly and without questioning His Word and a beautiful obedience brick is produced. Watch out!" he shouted, "here's another load arriving."

The young angel jumped out of the way as the shining golden bricks tumbled to the ground and the builders rushed to pick them up.

"Look! That was a phone call the King required," his mentor pointed out, "and that was an encouraging word someone needed to hear. That entire wall is made from promptings to pray. She obeyed instantly and more of these wonderful golden bricks arrived."

He turned to the other mansion, sparkling as though made from the finest diamonds.

"Each of these sparkling bricks is made from an act of love. Every time His handmaiden puts her arm around someone or cries with a hurting friend or spends an hour with a lonely neighbour or shares her belongings with the poor, the angels are sent these strong special bricks. The angels all love working on this site for the mansions reflect Heaven's Light so beautifully."

The young angel gazed around the site and laughed aloud in sheer delight,

"What a surprise these handmaidens are going to get when the King shows them their mansions! I hope I'm around to see their faces."

And the two angels flew off to present their report to the King of Heaven, the One whose Voice still calls handmaidens to serve Him in love and obedience.

OTHER BOOKS BY GLORIA KEARNEY

Sing in the Shadow

Special Moments

A Place Prepared

Sunrise to Sunset

Copies available by contacting Gloria at
gmjkearney@googlemail.com

Pat Logan can be contacted at
rlogan@talktalk.net